Dear Felicity

PASSING
the BATON

—— PETER RUCK ——

Love & blessings

Rick

21/7/23

British Library Cataloguing in Publication Data

A record for this book is available from the British Library

ISBN: 978-1-910719-64-0

Design by Verité CM Ltd
Print management by Verité CM Ltd
www.veritecm.com

Printed in England

PASSING
the BATON
—— PETER RUCK ——

When we pass the baton we must ensure a correct handover.

TONY JARRETT is a former sprint and hurdling athlete from England. He was a silver medalist in the 110 meters hurdles in the World Championship in 1993 and 1995 and at the European Championship in 1990. He won gold at the Commonwealth Games in 1998 and was a member of the men's 4 x 100m relay team at the World Championships in 1991 and 1993. Tony is also a four times Olympian.

'I press toward the mark for the prize of the calling of God in Christ Jesus' (Phillipians 3:14).

"Peter that picture is so powerful in so many ways. The vision you had for us to have this photograph taken together says so much. Here are some things that came into my mind.

- *Passing on our faith*
- *Knowing that our lives are in safe hands*
- *Passing on the baton to achieve the greater prize*
- *That we are all running in a race know matter what kind of background, culture or race.*

Congratulations on writing your first book. I can imagine the great stories you can tell and the wonderful works of God.

Blessings, Tony Jarrett"

Things to know, places to go and miracles to show will be sparked within you as you read the challenges that a man on a mission can encounter and overcome. This will help you as you go from stability to success to significance in your life because you have made a choice that God will back up. Enjoy the ride you get in the read.

Dr. Kevin McNulty

I have known Peter for many years and have always appreciated his heart for the Lord Jesus Christ. We have shared in a few projects together and, through His grace, there has always been a blessing. I would encourage you all to read his book mainly because it reminds us of just how much God is willing to work with and through us when we are genuinely open and available to Him. Be blessed.

Pastor Jem Trehern MA

Dear Peter, I've read your book and can say 'Well Done!' Thankful for your vision, faithfulness and passion in working tirelessly in many ways to mobilise the church to work together for the greatest cause... proclaiming Jesus to those who have never heard and seeing prodigals come home. Keep following His lead!

Revd. Gary Seithel MS

I have known my friend Peter for many years, and what you cannot miss is his passion for Christ and sincere desire to share the gospel with one and all. It is no wonder then that he operates under the banner of Zeal Outreach Ministries, which is a platform for prayer, intercession and thanksgiving and also serves to promote evangelism worldwide. I pray his story will touch you and inspire you to know Him for yourself and make Him known to others.

Joseph Mathai

DEDICATION

*To my wife Judy Choo-Ean who sent me to the Jungle where my mission work began
and who shares my desire to minister love to a hurting world*

and

*To family and friends who have encouraged and supported me
on my journey through life*

ACKNOWLEDGEMENTS

I want to give thanks to all my teachers, beginning with my parents. We know nothing we have not learned from a teacher or experienced in life. I am indebted to all who have taught me, both academically and spiritually. Truths gleaned from many sources have become a permanent part of my life and some of these surface in the book. Thank you to all those who passed the baton to me.

In particular I want to thank those who have supported me in my ministry, especially my home church where I was born-again 25 years ago, for the continued love and friendship I have enjoyed on the journey.

To those who encouraged me to write this book in the first place and continued to nag until I completed the task.

To my wife Judy for her patience during the writing process and providing "a word in season" when I flagged.

To Auntie D who over the years has poked many packets of black jacks and fruit salad sweets through my letter box and read the first draft of the book – red pen in hand.

To those who have read chapters of the text to verify my facts. Any errors that remain are down to me.

To Louise Stenhouse for editing the manuscript. To Chris Powell at Verité, whom I first met when I ran a printing business, for his help in printing and publishing the book.

Thank you all.

CONTENTS

INTRODUCTION

My passion is to encourage and tell everyone that life can be different. I spent most of my working life in business making huge promises of high standards at the lowest prices – but delivering on those promises depended on man. Now I have a different message that comes with a heavenly guarantee: 'JESUS our Healer, Provider, and Redeemer'. HE paid the price for you and me! 'IT'S A FREE GIFT.'

Yes, I am 'Peter Ruck, a man of second chances'; this is an ideal introduction for me. Psalm 23:4 sums up how God has been faithful to me throughout all my experiences: 'Yea, thou I walk through the valley of the shadow of death, I will fear no evil: for thou art with me; thy rod and thy staff they comfort me.' I am living proof HE cares about EVERYONE!

God has provided me with amazing opportunities to share this story.

Some time ago I was really challenged by the song 'You're the Only Jesus Some Will Ever See'. This became a reality when I had a wonderful opportunity to take the gospel deep into the rainforest jungle of Malaysia. God put this desire in my spirit a long time ago: 'Go ye into all the world and preach the gospel to every creature' (Mark 16:15). What has also proved to be true is 'You shall receive power when the Holy Spirit comes upon you' (Acts 1:8).

My fervent desire is to encourage those who already believe, and invite those who do not, to hear or read my story of God's goodness, grace and mercy proving that God is real.

God wants to empower us; the Lord wants all saved people to receive 'power from on high' (Luke 24:49). Power to witness, power to act, power to live and to show the divine manifestations of God within us. The power of God will take you out of your own plans and into HIS plan. The Lord will change you and put in His mind where yours was, and thus enable you to 'have the mind of Christ' (1 Corinthians 2:16). You will find yourself praying and seeking God's will. Well, that's the way it is for me. I am looking to do God's will under His anointing through the power of the Holy Spirit within. 'Do nothing out of selfish ambition or vain conceit. Rather, in humility value others above yourselves' (Philippians 2:3 NIV).

When I am unsure in any situation I find myself asking, 'What would Jesus do?' The answer is, 'Pray!' Prayer is so important. It is the key in my relationship of faith.

John 15:16 (NKJV) says, 'You did not choose Me, but I chose you and appointed you that you should go and bear fruit, and that your fruit should remain, that whatever you ask the Father in My name He may give you.' My own viewpoint about faith / prayer: accepting the idea that we have been chosen by Jesus to build His kingdom, living accordingly requires faith – and that is the faith we bring to prayer when seeking from God what we need to accomplish the task before us. When God's Spirit has full control then our anxieties pass away. If we live in the Spirit we live above our human nature. If we reach this place that God's Son said we had come into, we will always come into a place of peace.

I have really struggled to write this book; in fact I have made every excuse possible for why I shouldn't write this book. It was in Moscow on my sixty-fifth birthday when Kevin and Leslie McNulty spoke a word over me telling me I needed to write a book relating my experiences as an encouragement to others. My biggest hang up has been the use of the word 'I' because I read somewhere that you are no good until you have your 'I' knocked out of you!

'Don't copy the behaviour and customs of this world, but let God transform you into a new person by changing the way you think. Then you will learn to know God's will for you, which is good and pleasing and perfect.' (Romans 12:2 NLT)

However God eventually got me to a place where I had no excuse not to start what I had been told to do years before, so I pray that you will see through the 'I' to the wonderful things in God's plan that HE has allowed me to be a part of. The race of life is like a relay race: the important thing in the race is getting the baton to the finishing line. The baton is the message and the runners' job is to do their part as God's messengers taking the good news of the gospel where He sends them and passing the baton on.

I came across this hymn on the Singing the Faith website and it so exactly sums up my feelings that I wanted to share it. I am indebted to Laurence Wareing, the site's editor, for giving me permission to include it.

God Who Sets Us on a Journey

God who sets us on a journey
to discover, dream and grow,
lead us as you led your people
in the desert long ago;
journey inward, journey outward,
stir the spirit, stretch the mind,
love for God and self and neighbour
marks the way that Christ defined.
Exploration brings new insights,
changes, choices we must face;
give us wisdom in deciding,
mindful always of your grace;
should we stumble, lose our bearings,
find it hard to know what's right,
we regain our true direction
focused on the Jesus light.
End our longing for the old days,
grant the vision that we lack –
once we've started on this journey
there can be no turning back;
let us travel light, discarding
excess baggage from our past,
cherish only what's essential,
choosing treasure that will last.
When we set up camp and settle
to avoid love's risk and pain,
you disturb complacent comfort,
pull the tent pegs up again;
keep us travelling in the knowledge
you are always at our side;
give us courage for the journey,
Christ our goal and Christ our guide.

Words: Joy Dine (1937–2001) Copyright © Revd Mervyn Dine
Reproduced with permission. www.singingthefaithplus.org.uk

Chapter 1

ON THE RIGHT PATH

My life journey began in a small Essex village called Abridge. I was born in a 'prefab'. For those who are not familiar with what a 'prefab' is, they were intended as a temporary replacement for housing that had been lost during the Second World War. Parts of these small bungalows were manufactured (prefabricated) in various factories and erected on site. It was my parents' first home: a single-storey, flat-roofed building on a council housing estate. These particular council houses were rented to couples without children. It was very basic: a kitchen, a living room heated by an open coal fire, two bedrooms and a bathroom.

This village was very intimate, everyone knew everyone. Many families were related through the generations and it was a very friendly place. The centre of the village was the green, which was a large circular, grassy area separated from the houses by a road that ran all the way around it. The green was a playground to us children. There was a big oak tree with a rope hanging down for us to swing from. It's still there. The green was also our football pitch. We would put four jackets down for our goals and the kids would join in. Big kids and little kids, all together. The road was our running track for relay races. We amused ourselves; nobody had much in the way of toys. We would go off to the woods walking for miles, climbing trees, jumping ditches. In the summer we would go down to the River Roding to paddle and catch minnows in our fishing nets.

The village consisted of three pubs and a few shops. The outside world was accessible by the Number 10 bus that ran from Abridge to Aldgate in London. The highlight of the year was Bonfire Night. We would build a massive fire on the green and we made 'guys' to put on the top. The kids worked hard together, gathering stuff to burn. Parents would also get involved. We didn't have many fireworks in those days, but we pooled our resources; it was an event for the whole community. People came out to watch the fireworks and stood chatting around the fire. In the days following the bonfire we cooked jacket potatoes in the embers.

My mum, Gladys, was a local girl having been brought up in Lambourne, a village a mile up the road. She had attended the local school, as had most of my friends' parents. She was a fit lady. I can remember her showing me a watch she'd won for running. Later on I can remember her being in the local paper for winning the 'pancake race'. When I started writing this chapter she was ninety-three years old. I asked why she called me Peter. 'Your dad and I loved the name; it's from the Bible,' she said.

My dad, Lloyd John Ruck, was a great influence in my life. He was not only a devoted husband and father but also my friend. Dad was born in Canada and was brought up there until my grandparents moved back to  the UK when he was about fourteen years old. He was a quiet, well-educated man, very sincere and a devout Christian, a man of principle. I can't ever remember my dad using bad language. He was very hard-working and would work nights to earn extra money for his family. He loved his motorbike and I remember us going out as a family with me in the little seat in the back of the sidecar. Dad's dream was to own a car so he could take us out with my grandparents.

Mum got her answer to prayer: a new three-bedroom, brick-built house. She lived in that house for over sixty years. I recently had to clear the house and found Mum had kept everything, especially if it involved her family. It's been so helpful in confirming details of some of my trips and events.

Every Sunday morning my parents would take me to Sunday school where I loved to listen to the Bible stories. I can remember learning the Lord's

Prayer at an early age. My dad would pray with me. His own Bible had been presented to him as a prize in his own Sunday school days. I used that Bible for many years before returning it to my mum.

We went to church as a family and for a number of years I sang in the choir at Lambourne Church, until my voice broke. Leaving the choir was a great excuse to kick God into touch. I really didn't get too much from the preaching. I found it boring. I just wanted to play football or cricket every minute of the day! I played for my primary school team from the age of eight, against teams of eleven-year-olds. Then at eleven years of age I was selected from the best players in the local village schools to play in the district schools' team.

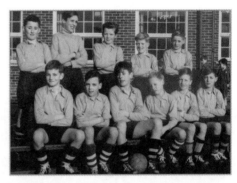

I went off to secondary school, an eight-mile bus ride to Ongar, and suddenly the cocoon I had been living in changed. What an awakening that was for me. I was one of a few kids turning up at 'big school' wearing shorts. It was like being amongst giants; some of the big kids were six feet tall. For the first time I was seeing how bullies operated, gathering kids around them to be in their 'gang'. It was cool to be seen smoking cigarettes behind the bike sheds! Fortunately, around this time my granddad caught me picking up his roll-up. He made me smoke it. I nearly choked; puffing at it almost made me sick. He said I looked green.

After Christmas in my first year at secondary school I was bought some long trousers. Although these were not great for playing football at break times they gave me the confidence to talk to girls. I was an only child and didn't know much about girls. I was starting to notice that they were different. I remember getting my first love letter from a girl signed, 'Love, Linda xxx SWALK'. Our friendship stayed like this until we were in the second year when we 'kissed'. I was naive.

My boyhood dream was to be a footballer. I was kicking a ball almost as soon as I had learned to walk. I was soon playing for the school teams not just in my year but also for the years above me. The school sent me off for trials for the Chelmsford & Mid-Essex Schools team at thirteen and I was picked for the side. Each week we had matches against teams from all over Essex and playing at this level attracted professional football scouts. Leyton Orient, then a First Division team, invited me to train with them twice a week. I got used to jumping on trains and buses carrying my kit and trying to do my homework. I was exposed to a different world, people's attitudes and language. It was quite a culture shock and I was so glad to have my dad to talk to. I didn't understand 'stuff' the lads and people were talking about in the dressing room. It made me feel uncomfortable.

My schoolwork suffered during the football season. My reports would always say 'could do better' and I moved from the A stream down to the B stream. My dad tried hard to motivate me with my schoolwork but playing sport was my life. Football and cricket kept me out of mischief most of time but I was very fit and started winning cross-country running races too. Football, however, was my focus. I would be kicking a football against the kerb playing 'push, run and turn' every day. I loved to talk to a professional player, John Lyall, who lived around the corner from us. John eventually became the manager of my favourite team West Ham United. As John was injured and not playing for the first team he began to coach young players. I told John it was my dream to play for West Ham, like him. I know he came over to the sports field to watch us local lads play in the evenings.

Being from Canada my dad didn't know much about football but he loved to support me. He wasn't happy about some of the 'stuff' I shared with him about conversations in the changing rooms and the crowd I was mixing with. He also was not happy about me travelling into Leyton by Underground and coming home in the dark, sometimes walking two miles home carrying my bags. He was working nights so he couldn't meet me off the train at Theydon Bois station. If the bus didn't arrive, I would have to walk.

My dad was a shy man so I was very surprised when he asked John Lyall, 'How can my son switch to West Ham?' Dad didn't know it but their scouts had already been to see me play several times.

John told him that the best thing he could do was to write to Wally St Pier, then the chief scout, and ask for a trial for me. That way he was making the approach 'legal' because I was already associated with the Orient. Within a few days Dad got a reply. When I got home one evening he said, 'Peter, there's a postcard inside.'

I was speechless!

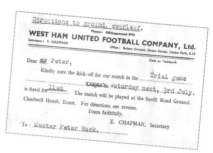

I had been invited to attend a trial on a Saturday morning. There must have been over a hundred young lads like me who had come from all over Great Britain; some of these lads were playing for England, Scotland, Wales and Ireland as international players. I was so nervous; we played for around half an hour and then got moved to another pitch, playing with a different bunch of lads each match. I played in three half games. We were told the club would write to us if we were successful. After three more trial weekends I was invited to train at Upton Park once a week. I was actually getting changed in the same dressing room as legends like Moore, Hurst and Peters!

It was a dream come true when I was picked to play in the junior and youth teams in the South Eastern Counties league, wearing the claret and blue shirt at Chadwell Heath, which was West Ham's training ground. I played there until I was almost eighteen and felt honoured to see my name in the match-day programmes and in the youth reports.

Then I got a letter from Wally St Pier saying I was not going to be offered an apprenticeship and the club wished me well. I was devastated.

I had started work as a commercial artist in a London advertising agency but the job didn't work out. A neighbour invited me to go and work for him in the print industry which set me on a path for the next fifty years. My new boss also loved football (albeit an Arsenal fan!) and he encouraged me to join non-league clubs. I played for both Chelmsford City and Romford youth sides, both were semi-professional. After a while the constant travelling to matches and practices wore me out and I became very disillusioned so I just played with my mates. Then I was invited to play with a new youth team in Chigwell which was being put together by an ex-Chelsea player. We won everything locally. I was soon given a nickname – Rucko – nobody was called by their own name. I learnt so much from our coach Jimmy Baverstock and I missed him greatly when he eventually emigrated to Australia. It was a very friendly team and we had great support from our families – our dads would come to all of our matches. We all became such close friends and once went on holiday to Italy together. Every weekend we went out together down to the pub or local dance halls, such as the Ilford Palais. On one of these Saturday nights I met a girl from East Ham called Eileen and we started seeing each other regularly.

Much as I enjoyed playing with the youth team, I was itching to play at a higher level again. Finally, I ended up playing for Clapton which, for several years, was a senior amateur club in the East End of London at the Spotted Dog Ground. My new girlfriend worked just around the corner in Plaistow as a nursery nurse in a children's home, as I discovered when I dropped her off in my little Morris Minor after a Saturday-night dance.

When I reflect back on my childhood, teenage and early-adult years, I am so grateful to both of my parents who sowed some solid principles into my life. My parents were both honest, hard-working, godly examples to me.

'Train up a child in the way he should go: and when he is old, he will not depart from it.' (Proverbs 22:6)

The Lord's Prayer is deeply rooted within me; I have continued to pray this prayer. I always say to myself, 'What would Jesus do?' He would go to the Father in prayer. As my story continues you'll see.

As I look back I can see God's hand on my life and this was the inspiration for me to produce a tract of a hand entitled 'Bringing You Good News'. On one side is the Lord's Prayer and on the other side is this scripture, *'See, I have inscribed you on the palms of My hands; your walls are continually before Me'* (Isaiah 49:16 NLT).

Chapter 2

NEW HORIZONS

A new chapter in life was beginning. I was working for a living and I had my own means of transport. I had been saving my money to buy a car since I was fifteen, working during the school holidays for Uncle George who was a turf contractor, rolling up turf in the fields. I would also pick mushrooms from the fields and go around selling them. I finally saved up £150 to buy a neighbour's Morris 1000. Living in a remote village having a car made a big difference. I could now get to work easily at the printing company. When I worked overtime I didn't have to worry about missing the last bus home at night. I could travel to East London for football training twice a week and then go on to meet my girlfriend Eileen at the nursery where she worked.

I would try to see Eileen a few times a week. Some of the other lads had girlfriends too by now and it suddenly changed from being an all-boys' scene. We would go out as groups of couples. I was smitten by Eileen; she was such a compassionate person. She loved the children in the nursery and the children loved her back. We would often take some of the kids to Plaistow Park or Wanstead Flats in the back of the car. I would get choked up when the kids would claim me to be their dad. When I called round for Eileen the kids would shout, 'It's my daddy!' Perhaps, unbeknown to me, that's when God first sowed the seed of ministering to children in my heart.

Suddenly Eileen became unwell. I went to her parents' house as she had been off sick all week. When I arrived her mum was waiting for the doctor. I remember Eileen being so thirsty we would carry jugs of water for her. She would down a pint of water like the lads drank their beer on a Friday night. I said I would come back to see her at the weekend.

I arrived at the weekend to learn she had been taken to hospital. I was really worried about her, thinking, 'God, I hope she's alright.' We had been seeing each other for six months by then and she had become such an important part of my life. She looked so unwell with a drip in her arm. The doctors told her she had diabetes and that she would have to have injections of insulin for the rest of her life. I remember saying to myself and speaking to God at the same time, 'God, please help her, I love her.' Eileen was so upset and kept saying to me that I would get fed up with her now. How wrong she was. I was frightened of losing her. I used all my savings to buy a ring so that I could propose to her. She said 'yes' and we were engaged to be married.

Eileen was such a brave girl; I'd never seen anyone sick before, let alone watched someone giving themselves injections! It scared me to watch her injecting herself but her grandparents encouraged me: 'Our Eileen, she's a tough girl. She climbed trees better than most boys!'

Sure enough, she had plenty of determination and was soon back working in the nursery again. We were in love, we just wanted to be together and get married. Neither of us was earning much money; she was very poorly paid and my job depended on overtime and a 'bit of boot money' (as amateur players, we couldn't be paid officially). Lack of funds didn't stop us; we got married on a shoestring in my village and our parents did the catering in the village hall. We had no money for a honeymoon until Eileen's granddad gave us some. I used it to book into a local bed-and-breakfast in Woodford for one night. On the Sunday morning we woke up as a married couple, ate scrambled eggs on toast, Eileen had her injection and we were off and ready to go!

We went to Wanstead Flats where I was playing in a semi-final of a Sunday morning football competition. The team won with my new wife there cheering us on! Lunch was back to my mum and dad's where we were going to live until we got our own home. Sunday afternoon we were off to the pictures. We watched *Till Death Us Do Part*. A really funny storyline based in the East End of London with an ironic title. I cringe when I think about this now, but we were happy!

I knew I needed to get a better job with the potential to earn more money, and I needed to reduce my outgoings. I worked in both the print shop and the photographic studio of the company. I saw an advertisement for a job as a trainee salesman of an international company, selling print and photographic materials. I was praying I would get this job as it offered a basic salary, commission on sales and a new company car with all the fuel paid for.

I got the job. My six months probationary period was cut to three and I was assigned to work in London. A new car was on its way and I was hungry for success.

Then Eileen told me she was pregnant. She was so excited; I was a little scared by the thought of the responsibility but it spurred me on. We sold the Morris 1000, keeping the money to one side for when we got our own home. My sales and commission were great, well above the company's expectations.

We moved out of my parents' house and rented a place of our own, and then we became parents when our son John was born prematurely. Dear Eileen had spent two months in hospital because of the diabetes and the baby was born by caesarean section. Eileen had to stay in hospital after the birth as John had jaundice and was in an incubator. But he was a big baby despite being a month and a half early. It was an exciting and scary time for me; I secretly prayed asking God for help! Finally Eileen was home with John; we were a family and she was an amazing new mum.

My job was going really well and my sales results were good. Our office manager had moved to a new American company and he asked me if I would be interested in talking to his boss about new opportunities. I took the job and was given a large area covering East Anglia, a big car, great basic salary plus commission and bonuses. I 'hit the ground running' and began to do really well.

Despite the new job the early years of our marriage were a struggle financially; even to buy coal and to pay the milkman every week we had to budget carefully. Everything was second-hand! Now we were planning to have a second child. We were hoping for a daughter. I was very nervous about Eileen becoming pregnant again as I had vivid memories of her spending time in hospital before and after the birth of our son John. I wanted another child but I was worried about Eileen. The doctors told us this should be our last child because of Eileen's health.

I know Eileen was praying for a daughter. She'd already decided in her head that the baby's name would be Susanne. I know my dad was really praying for a granddaughter too. Their prayers were answered. I can remember Eileen's grandparents with big grins on their faces saying to us that we had a 'pigeon pair'.

Life was running smoothly. The children were fine. Eileen was well and so enjoying being a mother. I had started a small business with a friend that I would do in the evenings after my daytime sales job. I was ambitious; I wanted to buy our own house, as we would soon need three bedrooms. I really needed to do this while I was still employed in order to get a mortgage. I was working all day and half the night. Our small business was starting to take off.

Then suddenly I had phone call from my mum. Dad was unwell; he had been rushed to hospital having had a heart attack. My world was in turmoil; he was my best friend as well as my dad. I remember praying, 'God, please make my dad well again.' It was such a shock as he was only fifty-three. Dad was very overweight, never seemed to show his frustrations and he seemed to take all life's situations in his stride. Now the doctors put him on a crash diet and an exercise regime. Bless him, he followed the doctors' instructions and was back to work within six months. I couldn't imagine living life without him!

Life went back to normal. We bought our first house and the business I started with a partner was going very well so I left my full-time job to become self-employed. My parents loved their grandchildren and they were a great support to us. I was working very long hours being 'driven by success'.

Two years later my father died. He was only fifty-five years old. He had a massive heart attack whilst at work. I was devastated, being the only child and still only twenty-four. It took me quite a time to come to terms with Dad's passing. I had to support my mum and I would call in to see her on my way to work in the morning and on my way home at night as she adjusted to being on her own.

Our business was expanding: from the original Litho plate makers we had branched out into a print and design company, and the printing side was

Chapter 3

STORMY CLOUDS AHEAD

D ark clouds were now on the horizon as pressure was coming thick and
fast both at home and at work.

Eileen's health began to deteriorate seriously and I was taking more and
more time off work to attend hospital appointments with her. The diabetes
was not always as stable as it should have been and the predictions were that
this would inevitably lead to further complications. She was referred to St
Bartholomew's Hospital (Bart's) in London for a consultation. The specialist
diagnosed the onset of kidney failure due to arterial problems that had already
led to her receiving laser treatment for her eyesight as a result of diabetes. It
was painful and distressing watching her like this. I know our children found
it hard. They had learnt to fend for themselves whilst growing up as a cold
or a tummy upset would make Eileen really ill.

It was around this time the recession started which was having a serious
effect on our business. People were cutting back on advertising spend and
our turnover was dropping month by month. We were losing money for the
first time! We had to cut our own salaries and make some people redundant.
It was the first time we'd had to do anything like this. It wasn't easy telling
people that you worked with every day that you could no longer afford to
employ them. One young man actually cried; another was angry.

The situation at work really troubled me. Normally at work I could focus
on the job and shut off what was going on at home. Now there was no
escape from the pressures and, from the stress of it all, I started to suffer from

headaches. I started to have a few whiskies when I got home from work to help me unwind. It became a vicious circle: alcohol was my solace from the pressure but alcohol increased the intensity of the headaches. What began as a couple of glasses progressed to half a bottle of whisky a night. I would wake up the next day feeling rubbish and with another headache, this one a self-inflicted hangover!

Living with this cloud hanging over us was very frustrating, especially for Eileen. By now our children had homes of their own so when I went to work in the morning all Eileen had for company was our faithful collie dog Lassie. I would leave for work each day not knowing how Eileen would be when I got home at night. She had such strength of character, a real fighter; she would have to be really unwell not to have a dinner ready for me. Lassie was Eileen's protector and her best friend, watching out for her twenty-four hours a day. If Eileen went to the kitchen the dog would get up and follow her. Any sign of distress and she would get up and bark, even if Eileen only coughed. If anyone came to the door Lassie would be up at the front door standing in front of Eileen. That dog was so sensitive and had such a perception of the situation.

We needed a break and as things had levelled out a bit at work we decided to go to the Lake District. We booked a lovely cottage where we could enjoy the scenery. I could drive Eileen around sightseeing without putting her through any physical stress. Then she became really unwell. I had to call for an ambulance and she was rushed to Carlisle hospital where she was immediately admitted. We were told her kidneys were in failure and she would need dialysis. The hospital talked of transferring her to Newcastle hospital where they had a kidney unit. I telephoned the children and they drove the three hundred miles to be with us at the weekend. The consultant in Carlisle spoke with the consultant at Bart's who suggested that Eileen's condition was stable enough to allow her to travel, so we drove back to London ourselves.

I felt very nervous at the thought of driving back home with her alone. My instructions were to take her straight to the hospital in London as they would need to put her on a list for continuous ambulatory peritoneal dialysis (CAPD). This meant an operation to put a tube into her abdomen to allow her to receive dialysis at home. Once the wound had healed enough we were both trained so that when she came out of hospital I could help and support her. By the end of the day she was often too tired to carry out the final dialysis treatment and then it would be up to me to drain and replace the dialysis bag for her whilst she slept. The continuous hospital visits and laser treatment on her eyes were really getting to her; she lost her appetite and was becoming depressed.

I was continually encouraging her, reminding her of the song 'Come on Eileen', but she was losing that spark that drove her on and could not be left on her own all day.

My escape from the situation was to wait until she had fallen asleep and nip around the corner to the pub for a couple of pints with my friend Jack. Then I would come home and down a few more whiskies – some nights it was half a bottle, on one occasion it was a whole bottle – and then I would fall asleep in the chair. I became irritable and frustrated; drinking was my way of dealing with the situation and it wasn't working. I felt hopeless. I was finding it harder and harder to encourage Eileen because the situation was gripping me. When I could, I went out to play golf or to Freemasonry lodge meetings. I seized any opportunity and it normally ended up with a drinking session. I didn't know which way to turn. Working hard and money had been my answers for solving problems in life but they weren't working now. I was truly desperate. Then we received invitations from one of Eileen's relatives to watch a video from a church where she had attended a carol concert the previous year. The video featured a man who gave a testimony of how his blind eye was 'miraculously' opened following prayer.

Desperation brings a 'diversion to seek hope' in a hopeless situation. Eileen had kidney failure and she was totally depressed by the other predicted health issues hanging over her. I was feeling out of control. We went along to the church but didn't receive the prayer we hoped for. What we did receive was a lot of love, warmth and friendship from the people attending this 'happy clappy' church. Just as we were leaving, a lady sitting close by said, 'Come along again on Tuesday night – I'm sure the pastor will pray with you.' It was just before Christmas.

On Christmas Day 1992 we were eating Christmas dinner with our daughter Susanne when Eileen suddenly cried out, 'I can't see! Everything has gone black.' There was silence around the table, everyone was in such shock. You can imagine our tears as we could only stand up and hug her.

We had been told by the hospital this would happen and nothing could be done. But when it actually did happen it was devastating. We knew this church had a midweek service after Christmas so we decided together it was our best hope to go and ask for prayer.

In our hopeless situation we asked the minister to pray and ask God for help for all Eileen's medical problems. When we entered the church Eileen was desperately depressed and full of fluid because she needed dialysis for her kidneys. There was no miraculous healing but what was evident was the prayer had brought hope; you could see a little smile on Eileen's face. The minister asked us to come again; this time I didn't need persuading. 'We will!' I was very open to go to church rather than playing golf next Sunday morning.

Reflection:

Sorrows and God's hope: pain is temporary, God is forever.

Chapter 4

DECISION TO TAKE A NEW PATH

Sunday morning came. This was new; we weren't used to going to church. The service started at 10.30 a.m. but I would normally have been on the first tee by 9. It was a half-hour drive from home to church but I only had to get my dad's old Bible and help Eileen get ready and guide her to the car. We arrived a little late to be greeted by friendly faces and the sound of lively music. As we walked in people were singing, clapping in time to the music and raising their hands.

'Not for us,' I thought. It was so different from my experience as a boy in the Anglican church. I could see, however, that Eileen was enjoying the music, she loved the lively tempo. That first Sunday I found myself watching rather than getting involved. At the end of the service people came over to talk to us. This was very different from my previous experience of church where people stayed in their pews.

We were back for more the following Sunday. This time I began listening to this straight-talking man on the platform, Pastor Michael Reid. He was very blunt and direct. It seemed everything was being directed towards me. Whilst I was listening I began having strange feelings in my body; it was hot and I felt quite disorientated, as if the room was spinning around. I told Eileen how I felt; she said she was enjoying being in church, especially how friendly everyone was. She was wearing dark glasses and, being blind, the fact that everyone seemed to know our names by the second week really made a big impression on her.

A week later we were on the same road going back again for more. Now I was being so challenged by everything the pastor was preaching from the Bible that I found myself talking to God. I wasn't just talking, I was arguing with God, telling Him, 'I am not here for me, it's for my wife. Can't You see how sick she is?' I was getting more and more angry but there was a conversation going on between God and me. The more the minister was speaking, the more I was getting challenged as I knew it was truth being spoken and it applied to me. Wow! Then I felt the power of God come on me and I couldn't struggle. My arms became so heavy I could hardly stand. The room seemed to be spinning around as if I had drunk too much whisky. While this was happening, I could hear the Word of God as it was spoken, every word was challenging me more and more! The pastor had made an appeal that anyone who wanted to repent and turn to follow Jesus should leave his or her seat and come forward. I knew that included me but, gripping the seat with my eyes closed, I said to God, 'How can I leave Eileen sitting here?'

I opened my eyes; the pastor seemed to be looking straight at me. A voice inside me was saying GO!

Decision made, I let go of the seat and began to walk through a number of people standing in front of the platform. The pastor began to pray for everyone as we responded to the call to follow Jesus. The power on me was more powerful than ever. I could hardly stand on my feet. The next moment the minister held my hand and that power intensified. I fell backwards to the floor (slain by the Holy Spirit). My body seemed to drain of the tension and anger I was carrying around. As I stood up I could feel tears running down my cheeks and a tremendous sense of peace as the 'burdens' seemed to be lifted off me. People were smiling at me and I was beginning to feel happy and joyful. It was like I was walking on air! My whole body remained on fire. It wasn't frightening; I just felt so happy and peaceful. I had never felt peace like this before. After twenty-five years it still remains the most wonderful day of my life – the day I was born again on 31st January 1993.

I will always be grateful for how He brought me out of the 'pit' I was living in. He gave me a new life; I was born again and filled by His Holy Spirit, there and then. I walked around with fire burning inside me for months. I still continue to feel that passion and fire within me even after twenty-five years of ministry, especially when praying or ministering to people. When

I'm 'laying hands' on someone in prayer I can sense God's power. They will tell me they're getting hot. What an amazing journey God continues to take me on day by day!

As I reflect on this chapter I can remember the immediate impact on my life. It was a life-changing day when I first knew the presence of God. I was beginning to feel the impact of the Holy Spirit; to feel the peace, love and joy. People I met were asking, 'What's happened to you?'

> *'Come to me, all you who are weary and burdened, and I will give you rest. Take my yoke upon you and learn from me, for I am gentle and humble in heart, and you will find rest for your souls. For my yoke is easy and my burden is light.'* (Matthew 11:28–30 NIV)

> *'But the fruit of the Spirit is love, joy, peace, forbearance, kindness, goodness, faithfulness.'* (Galatians 5:22 NIV)

The Roman Road

The scriptures that the pastor preached from that day were a series of verses from the book of Romans. I always carry them inside my Bible as a bookmark. This is the message I heard; it was so applicable to me. I am led to share the same message today!

This is a great overview from All About GOD Ministries.[1]

The Roman Road: A Well-engineered Path to Salvation

The Roman Road is a collection of verses in Paul's Epistle to the Romans that offers a clear and structured path to Jesus Christ. Although many people believe they will go to heaven because they have lived a good life, done charity work, been baptised as a child, attended church, or treated others fairly, the Bible declares that none of us can live up to God's standards of righteousness. Therefore, we need a road to God that doesn't rely on anything we do but, rather, relies on the gift of His grace alone.

The Roman Road: Follow this Map

The Roman Road provides a detailed map for our salvation and eternal fellowship with God. Just follow these steps:

1. We must acknowledge God as the Creator of everything, accepting our humble position in God's created order and purpose.

'For since the creation of the world His invisible attributes are clearly seen, being understood by the things that are made, even His eternal power and Godhead, so that they are without excuse, because, although they knew God, they did not glorify Him as God, nor were thankful, but became futile in their thoughts, and their foolish hearts were darkened.' (Romans 1:20–21 NKJV)

2. We must realise that we are sinners and that we need forgiveness. None of us are worthy under God's standards.

'For all have sinned and fall short of the glory of God.' (Romans 3:23 NKJV)

3. God gave us the way to be forgiven of our sins. He showed us His love by giving us the potential for life through the death of His Son, Jesus Christ.

'But God demonstrates His own love toward us, in that while we were still sinners, Christ died for us.' (Romans 5:8 NKJV)

4. If we remain sinners, we will die. However, if we repent of our sins, and accept Jesus Christ as our Lord and Saviour, we will have eternal life.

'For the wages of sin is death, but the gift of God is eternal life in Christ Jesus our Lord.' (Romans 6:23 NKJV)

5. Confess that Jesus Christ is Lord and believe in your heart that God raised Him from the dead and you are saved.

'That if you confess with your mouth the Lord Jesus and believe in your heart that God has raised Him from the dead, you will be saved. For with the heart one believes unto righteousness, and with the mouth confession is made unto salvation.' (Romans 10:9–10 NKJV)

6. There are no other religious formulas or rituals. Just call upon the name of the Lord and you will be saved!

'For "whoever calls on the name of the LORD shall be saved."' (Romans 10:13 NKJV)

7. Determine in your heart to make Jesus Christ the Lord of your life today.

'For of Him and through Him and to Him are all things, to whom be glory forever. Amen.' (Romans 11:36 NKJV)

The Roman Road: Are You Ready?

The Roman Road shows you the path – are you ready to accept God's gift of salvation now? If so, believe in what Jesus Christ did for you on the cross, repent of your sins, and commit the rest of your life to Him. This is not a ritual, just a prayerful guideline for your sincere steps of faith:

> 'Father, I know that I have broken Your laws and my sins have separated me from You. I am truly sorry, and now I want to turn away from my past sinful life towards You. Please forgive me, and help me avoid sinning again. I believe that Your Son, Jesus Christ, died for my sins, was resurrected from the dead, is alive, and hears my prayer. I invite Jesus to become the Lord of my life, to rule and reign in my heart from this day forward. Please send Your Holy Spirit to help me obey You, and to do Your will for the rest of my life. In Jesus' name I pray. Amen.'

'Repent, and let every one of you be baptised in the name of Jesus Christ for the remission of sins; and you shall receive the gift of the Holy Spirit.' (Acts 2:38 NKJV)

If you decided to receive Jesus today after reading this, welcome to God's family.

As we continue you will see how my life has been transformed.

[1] The Roman Road www.allaboutgod.com/the-roman-road.htm

Chapter 5

YOU'LL NEVER WALK ALONE

I became a Christian on Sunday 31st January 1993 at about mid-day. I went into my company on the Monday morning and began by telling my business partner. Then I told him, 'I have to change the way I am living my life – that means at home and at work. I need to tell everyone here at the factory.' He didn't object to me having a meeting with the staff and explaining what had happened over the weekend. Initially everyone was really shocked, especially when I removed all the pin-ups from the walls. I was no longer swearing, which was a huge departure from the usual culture in the printing industry. The change in me was very dramatic. People began to ask me questions; people were beginning to ask my partner and staff, 'What's happened to Peter?' My old friends, people I played golf with, friends I went to the pub with, business connections, all thought I had 'lost the plot'.

I didn't care what people thought. I was filled with a boldness to tell people what God had done for me.

Eileen wasn't verbal like me. She never really said much but she was a fighter, she caught people's attention by her dogged attitude. She was so pleased I'd had this encounter with God and she was now able to reveal her long-held fear that I would get fed up of her constant ill health. She knew both of the children were feeling the pressure of her being continually unwell. She had felt so alone, with very few true friends. Now we began to attend the midweek Bible study and the love and fellowship was a great encouragement to her.

Our children immediately saw the impact on my life as my heavy drinking came to a halt. The change for Eileen was a little more gradual but none the less dramatic. Eileen received prayer every week but in fact, she told me later, God had answered one of her prayers right at the beginning – that we could find something we could do together. Her faith was quietly growing stronger. Eileen was feeling loved and was making new friends of her own (normally new acquaintances to the family came through my connections).

Eileen said, 'I just want people to accept and want me for who I am.' She was changing, opening up, beginning to share things she had kept private, things dating back to her childhood. God was touching her whole being; hope came back into her life. In finding God she had found herself and had such peace within, knowing with absolute certainty that God loved her.

As a trained nursery nurse she absolutely loved children – it was her gift. She became friends with Lucie who ran the church crèche and Lucie invited Eileen to come and do voluntary work with her. It was such an encouragement for Eileen to feel wanted and useful again. Lucie would drive the fifteen miles to collect Eileen and bring her back home at the end of the day – sixty miles of driving for Lucie with never anything but a smile on her face. Working in the crèche Eileen made more friends and her self-esteem was returning along with her joy for life. Later I got to meet Lucie's husband Simon and their family at their home, and there I discovered something else: everyone was praying for Eileen, it wasn't just the church ministry team on a Sunday.

'You'll Never Walk Alone'

This song was originally written for the 1945 musical *Carousel* and a succession of artists, including Frank Sinatra and Elvis Presley, have subsequently recorded it. The version I grew up with was by Gerry and the Pacemakers and the lyrics describe so well how the life-changing meeting with God was for our family.

It was on 10th February 1993 and I was travelling to the NEC in Birmingham with my business partner. We had printed some greetings cards that were being exhibited so we were off to see the launch. It was a great opportunity for Brian and I to talk on the journey. I asked him if he minded if I played some of the Christian music from a tape that had been produced by the church I was attending. I began to tell him that I had found a real peace in my life and that Eileen was happier. He knew the tremendous stress I felt seeing her so sick. He didn't really make any comments, he just listened.

Then our conversation went something like this:

Me: 'Brian, I no longer have any fear of death.'

Brian: 'I don't either but I don't need God for that.'

Me: 'Really? If you could see this car hurtling towards a tree and we were going to hit it head on, I can tell you, you would be praying to God, "Please help me."'

I can remember telling Brian once again that I had no fear of death. What happened a few minutes later was incredible. We were in my new Mercedes 300 SEL driving in the centre lane of the M1 motorway at around 60mph, just going with the flow of traffic. It was 10 a.m. and the motorway was very busy. Suddenly 'CRASH!' We were spinning forward and sideways, propelled out of control as the large twelve-wheeled articulated lorry we were passing pulled out. Then another 'CRASH' as the lorry hit us again. There was the sound of metal vibrating and glass breaking and the smell of rubber. The second impact seemed to slow us up and sent us hurtling in a different direction between two lorries and towards the nearside crash barrier. Somehow, we had squeezed between them without either of them hitting us.

When the car came to a halt the bonnet was squashed up in front of the windscreen, or rather where the windscreen should have been – it had popped out and shattered. Remarkably there was not a scratch on either of us. I looked across and Brian was just looking straight forward, transfixed.

'Brian, are you OK? Brian, are you OK? Brian! Brian!' He didn't answer me.

I managed to open my door, get myself out of the car and walk round to the passenger side. Opening the door, I said, 'Brian, are you OK?'

Eventually he was able to answer, 'Yes!'

By now the traffic had stopped and motorists and lorry drivers came rushing to see if we were OK. We were standing against the crash barrier in a state of deep shock looking at our crumpled car.

It was a French lorry driver who had hit us. He hadn't stopped; in fact he hadn't seen us. The driver of the lorry behind the French vehicle had stopped

him a little further up the motorway and walked him back to the scene of the accident.

The second lorry driver said, 'It was a miracle how I didn't drive straight into you. I didn't miss you; somehow you slid between the two lorries.' He had been following the French articulated lorry when it pulled out without warning. By now the police had arrived and they had so many witnesses to confirm how the accident had occurred. The police told me that, as the driver, I needed to decide if the lorry was being driven dangerously. If so, as he hadn't stopped, the driver would be arrested, taken to a local police station and put in a cell.

The French lorry driver apologised in broken English and said that he hadn't seen us. The traffic police confirmed that it was quite common for left-hand-drive lorries to have a blind spot. They also said that his documents were in order and it would be very difficult to bring charges against the driver but that if we wanted to do so we would need to accompany them to the police station.

The ambulance had arrived and the paramedics gave us a quick check over. We decided to let the police take us to a local hotel to wait for my son John to come and drive us back to Essex. It wasn't until we were driving home that the whiplash injuries became evident and John took us to the local hospital.

Eileen was so relieved to see me walk through the door. She said, 'I have been praying for you and Brian.' God had miraculously kept us safe; we hadn't been alone. Eileen and I prayed together – a prayer of thanksgiving for His keeping hand.

Chapter 6

EYES OPENED AND A NEW DIRECTION

I believed God was leading me in a new direction. I remember reading the scripture: 'But seek ye first the kingdom of God and his righteousness; all these things shall be added unto you' (Matthew 6:33). I was witnessing different styles of ministry from my boyhood experiences of church.

At church I began to hear some great speakers such as Archbishop Benson Idahosa from Nigeria. The archbishop had a prophetic and a miracle ministry and was a renowned preacher around the world. He spoke with authority and boldness and seemed larger than life. God used him in a way I had never seen before. He was a regular visitor to the church in Brentwood and was speaking there when I went to the church for the first time.

I was sitting next to Eileen at a service in early 1993 when the archbishop turned around, looked directly at me, pointed at me and said in an extremely loud voice, 'Brother, you are called to be an encourager. God is telling you now to be an encourager all the days of your life.'

I knew this was God speaking to me. When God speaks it makes an impression on a person.

In a service one Sunday the archbishop said, 'Do you know what the devil's biggest weapon is? It's not sickness and diseases; it is discouragement!' This really resonated with me. I knew I was called to encourage the people that I met. Over the years God has widened my horizons so that wherever I am in the world, I encourage people that Jesus is our healer, our redeemer and that He set us free on the cross.

I met Dr Judson Cornwall, a Bible teacher from Arizona in the USA. I couldn't get enough of hearing this Spirit-filled gospel teacher. He spoke with such clarity and gentleness. I was invited to join him on a flight to France, to accompany him when he was going for the dedication and opening of a new church in Elverdinge, Belgium. It was such a privilege to be able to spend time talking with someone who had so much experience in the things of God. Some months later I met another American Evangelist, Billy Burke; a very charismatic preacher, who gave words of knowledge and had a real healing gift. It was an eye-opener for me to see how these men operated in the giftings of God.

My priorities in life were changing. Things that had been my focus now seemed unimportant. The 'bigger and better' attitude I had because of the success of my business was no longer a driving force in my life.

My friends had got used to me not swearing when I sliced or hooked a golf shot. I was no longer a big drinker, the one who was always ready to go to the pub. Playing golf and social events were less of a draw; my lifestyle change meant it wasn't easy to join in with some of the blokeish conversations. The home that Eileen and I had literally built together seemed less important to us now.

I was a Freemason and through the lodge I had met some really sincere people and made some great friends. I was organising a charity appeal to buy televisions for Bart's Hospital Kidney Unit for the patients having dialysis. But now I had become uncomfortable each time I went to the lodge meetings. I liked the people, but I began to feel uncomfortable in my spirit. It felt so wrong being part of this secret society but I couldn't put my finger on why.

Then one Sunday morning a scripture reading in church included the verse: 'Jesus answered, "I am the way the truth and the life. No one comes to the Father except through me"' (John 14:6 NIV). The scripture spoke directly to my unease about my membership of the Freemasons. Suddenly it was so clear. When I was interviewed to become a Freemason, I had been asked if I believed in a Supreme Being, and I said, 'Of course.' Now I knew what was making me feel so uncomfortable. Masons would accept any god and didn't ask questions. Although they were good, kind, charitable men, being a

Mason didn't seem to match up with God's Word. In fact, it seemed opposed to God's Word and to my faith.

So I went to my sponsors at the lodge with my questions. Why was Jesus never mentioned? They could not answer me. They only tried to justify the fraternity by saying that members of the royal family, judges, bishops and other dignitaries were Masons.

I had nothing against anyone as an individual but I could not 'fellowship' with them any more in the temple. They reluctantly accepted my resignation and, during my final lodge meeting, I was allowed to address the members openly about my reasons for resigning. I told them what I believed God had said to me. I quoted the scripture He had given me. I told them I felt that being a Freemason was incompatible with what God had called me to. I promised to honour my commitment to the charity event at Bart's Hospital until the end of the year as I thought this was the right thing to do. The majority accepted my position and wished me well.

Eileen's Miracle

The miracle happened in church on a Sunday morning during the worship. The words of the hymns were projected onto a big screen – black text on a white background.

Eileen touched my arm, 'Peter, I can see light and the words!'

'You can see?'

'Yes, I can see your face but it's a bit blurry.'

She explained that at first she had begun to see light and then the black text had become visible. Her blind eyes opened – what an amazing miracle! What joy after the desolation of being totally blind on Christmas Day. Praise God it was an answer to all our prayers.

We returned to the hospital to tell them the news. They examined Eileen and said that due to the improved condition of the eyes they could now

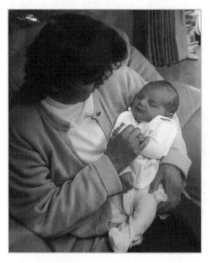

give her laser treatment that would, they hoped, prevent any more haemorrhages occurring.

Eileen received this miracle in the spring of 1993. As she dealt with all the problems arising from the complications of diabetes she said, 'I just pray that I can see for as long as I live.' God answered her prayer. She was thrilled that she could see her first grandson when he was born just before Christmas almost a year after she lost her sight.

A Passion to Share Good News

On another Sunday morning in those early days, I was sitting in church when a message was preached which seemed, once again, to be one of those moments when God was speaking directly to me.

'He said to them, "Go into all the world and preach the gospel to all creation."' (Mark 16:15 NIV)

It was a message that gave me a passion and purpose; in fact, it totally changed my life. I had already begun to share the love of Jesus on the local streets, at work – in fact anywhere I got a chance to have a conversation. One of the earliest opportunities came when I bought four company cars from a local car dealer. I was talking to the dealership principal, Kevin. He asked, 'How are you enjoying your new cars?'

I said that they were a bit different from my Mercedes.

'Yes, I am sure you've noticed the difference in your fuel costs!'

'Kevin, I have my story in this church newspaper. Can I give you a copy to read? It not only tells you about the miraculous way God saved me when I was involved in a terrible car crash, but how God opened my wife's blind eyes! It's the insurance money from the Mercedes that paid for these cars.'

Kevin took the paper, probably as much to keep a customer happy than with any intention of reading it! Can you imagine what a thrill it was when Kevin and his wife came to church? God can use any means to get a person's attention.

Now I felt God was challenging me to do more than simply share my story with the individuals that I met in everyday life or on the high street. I needed to broaden my outlook and take His message further afield.

God's plans are not our plans and sometimes we have to take the unexpected paths which open before us, even though we don't know, at the time, where they will lead.

The Sunday that Kevin and his wife first came to church was the day after our Silver Wedding dedication so, ironically, we were not there to talk with them, but I met up with him the following week. In a short time we became very good friends and began to serve together in local outreach ministry. This was another step along the path of evangelism. Was our meeting merely coincidence? No, I believe it was part of God's plan.

I just love sharing my faith and what Jesus did for me. I know God has put this on my heart, to share His wonderful love with many hurting people. I am sure from what you've read so far you can understand why I know we all need a heavenly Father who loves us unconditionally. You can't buy that peace and you can't earn it.

Reflection:

'For God so loved the world that he gave his one and only Son, so that whoever believes in him shall not perish but have eternal life.' (John 3:16 NIV)

'With man this is impossible, but with God all things are possible.' (Matthew 19: 26 NIV)

Chapter 7

CALLED HOME

God took Eileen home on 18th May 1995 and each year at this time I reflect with a great sense of peace on how God walks us through these times and that He never leaves us. I think of how He prepares a table before us. For Eileen it was an assured destination in heaven. But as God prepared Eileen, He also prepared me, through her.

A week before she died we were on our way to church when Eileen said, 'Stop here, Peter, I want to talk you.'

I pulled the car into a lay-by at the side of the road.

'What do you want to talk about?'

'I want you to promise me something. Firstly, I want you to promise me that you'll carry on going to church.'

'Of course I will.'

'OK!' Eileen said. 'Now, secondly, when you're ready, promise me you'll find someone to spend your life with when I am gone'

I wasn't ready for this stop in the lay-by. But as we talked we both sensed that God was calling her home. Normally I would be saying, 'Come on, Eileen!' but this time she had such an amazing peace about her and I sensed she felt completely in control. She didn't often speak to me about her faith but now, in her very being, I could feel it. It was an amazing witness. This was such a personal moment between us that I didn't feel I could share it with anyone at that time.

Eileen had become increasingly unwell and found it very difficult coping with the kidney failure. She was deteriorating so quickly that she was admitted to hospital in London. She could no longer tolerate the home dialysis. She was in the high dependency unit where her kidney function and blood sugar levels could be monitored constantly. I was spending most of each day at her bedside. I was exhausted. The doctors and nurses told me I needed to take a break and our friend Simon, who had driven up to London to visit, suggested that he collect me after visiting that evening and take me away overnight to spend the next day fly-fishing in Hampshire. I slept for the entire journey. The next day we both caught the largest rainbow trout of our lives and I was looking forward to telling Eileen my fisherman's tale.

In the afternoon we headed back to London and I was still so tired I slept most of the way back. Just as we were approaching London my mobile rang; it was the ward sister saying Eileen was unwell. I told her that we would be there shortly and then I called the children to come to the hospital. Then we had another call from the ward sister to say that Eileen had suffered a stroke. We were just a few minutes away and as soon as we arrived I ran up the stairs to the ward. The medical team was standing at the entrance to the ward. The sister said, 'I'm sorry, Peter, Eileen passed away peacefully just after I called you'.

Our children arrived not long after and I had to break the news to them that their mum had died. Whilst we all knew she had been very ill it was still a shock, especially for John and Susanne. It was the end of a long journey with many trials for Eileen but even in hospital she had, in her quiet way, been a witness of her faith as evidenced by the number of medical staff who came from London to attend her thanksgiving service.

Eileen always had two favourite songs in her mind: 'Oh Come and Meet the Great Redeemer' and her absolute favourite 'We Believe', which summed up both her belief and the awesomeness of God. She loved Psalm 23, the words of which were an inspiration and a comfort to us both. All these were included in the service.

It was a tremendous loss to us all. Eileen was a courageous lady, a good mother and wife, whom God finally called home to give her a glorified body and to fulfil His promise of eternal life. She was truly 'born again'. I am often asked and challenged about miracles. I remember a discussion with a minister whose viewpoint was that miracles happened when Jesus walked the earth but they don't happen today. All I could say to him was, 'My wife was blind and God opened her blind eyes. She continued to see until the day God called her home.' This is a testimony of God's miraculous intervention. No one will ever persuade me otherwise and I will always give HIM the praise and the glory for His mercy, grace and loving kindness.

Chapter 8

MOVING FORWARD
IN A NEW DIRECTION

A s you can imagine, life without Eileen was very difficult at the beginning. It was hard going back to an empty house. I was used to living a set path: the lifestyle of a husband, a carer and a dad. Hard as it was for me, it had been much more difficult for the children who had watched their mother battle with illness for all of their lives and it was devastating to finally lose her. The children were both married with their own homes so we were not able to give each other much support. I remember reading a scripture: *'Trust in the LORD with all your heart; do not depend on your own understanding. Seek his will in all you do, and he will show you which path to take'* (Proverbs 3:5–6 NLT). I knew that I had to move forward with my life. I still had a business to run, people were depending on me for their livelihoods and the recession was still affecting our trade very badly.

The change in my life was taking me to Brentwood more and more during the week as well as at weekends. I was now able to get involved with the choir, which was a great opportunity to mix with people in the church. Some Saturday nights I helped with the youth group. I was invited to go fly-fishing and play golf. Simon and Lucie often invited me to stay over. Many other members of the church invited me to meals in their homes. God was finding ways to fill my free time.

I was beginning to find my way again. I went on a church holiday to Cornwall where I went horse riding for the first time in my life, played a few rounds of golf and went sightseeing with Leo from Holland, who had also recently become a widower. It was a good time of getting to know people.

On my visits to Simon and Lucie's home I would often see their neighbour Judy, who would sometimes pop round for a chat and a cup of tea. Sometimes Judy would invite us over for a meal and she was an excellent cook. Over time I got to know her and her teenage son Kevin quite well. Just before the church holiday to Cornwall, Simon and Lucie held a barbecue and Judy and I were among the guests. I asked if she was going on the holiday but she said that she would be working and she had her son at home. After the barbecue we stayed on to watch a movie; it wasn't a particularly romantic film but in the dark I found myself holding her hand.

Whilst I was away we were contacting each other regularly and I invited her out for a midweek meal when I returned. I enjoyed my time away all the more for having the meal with Judy to look forward to on my return. We had a really good evening and we started to see each other regularly and very quickly realised that we had fallen in love.

My friend Kevin decided to help the romance along. His family lived in a large house in Brentwood and they had a spare room.

'Come and live with us then you won't have to keep driving back home every night.'

They made me so welcome and I soon became part of their family, being 'Uncle Pete' to the children. Breakfast times, before we went our separate ways to work and school, were busy but so precious. Living in Brentwood was part of my 'moving on'. I had many interesting conversations with the youngsters and I was soon referring to Kevin and his wife as 'Mum and Dad'. It was a fun time. One thing the children did not like was egg for breakfast so one day I went into town and bought an egg poacher. The next morning at breakfast I announced that we would be having flying-saucer eggs that day.

'Mum, we've got flying-saucer eggs today,'

'Flying-saucer eggs, Uncle Pete?'

'Yes, we can have two each!'

'Flying-saucer eggs?'

'Yes!'

The problem of the kids eating eggs for breakfast was solved.

Kevin had just been given his first solo part with the choir and he would get nervous each time the choir was due to perform the song. I teased him mercilessly by standing outside the bathroom and singing his first line: 'Have you ever been hungry?' We loved to share banter with one another. It was definitely in God's plan to bring us closer and serve in the Kingdom of God together.

I lived with Kevin and his family for around a year before Judy and I got married. To this day I tease Judy by telling people that she would see me visiting Simon and Lucie then she would begin cooking one of her delicious meals and open the door so that the wonderful aroma would waft across the garden fence to draw me over! Just like the old saying: 'the way to a man's heart is through his stomach'.

We got married in our church on 12th April 1997. Judy was born in Malaysia although she is of Chinese origin and her full name is Judy Choo-Ean. I love this name, and often call her by it as it means 'pearly wave'. Her family: her mother and four brothers, were all in Malaysia and none of them were able to come to the wedding. Simon stood in as father of the bride – he and Lucie had, after all, been instrumental in bringing us together. Judy knew exactly what she wanted as far as wedding planning went. She is a great organiser and hostess and I was only allowed to know some of the details beforehand. It was to have an 'oriental flavour' so the guys wore oriental shirts and black dinner suits, the bridesmaids were in oriental-style handmade dresses. The wedding march was an oriental composed theme, and then in walked my future wife looking absolutely stunning in a red Chong San dress. It really made me turn my head.

It was amazing how our wedding came together so perfectly. So many people helped us in so many ways. It was a real blessing. We both wanted two songs and the reading of Psalm 23 in the service. The first hymn was 'O Lord my God, when I in awesome wonder' with the marvellous refrain 'How great thou art'. This song and this psalm continue to be so significant in our lives. We walked out to an up-tempo song – 'God is good all the time' – because He is; He is there with us in every situation.

Once Judy and I were married I sold my beautiful house in Theydon Bois. The only thing I thought I would miss was watching the deer in the sanctuary that backed on to the garden. Guess what? The outlook is just as splendid in Brentwood – we have wild deer and a forest at the bottom of the garden.

That Christmas I went to Malaysia for the first time. Judy had organised a Chinese banquet to celebrate with her family and friends. She wore that stunning red dress again. It was a special time and an opportunity for me to meet her family and for them to find out whom Judy had married.

Christmas in Malaysia was very different from how I was used to celebrating it in the UK. Malaysia is predominately a Muslim country and Christmas was only really celebrated in hotels, mainly for the tourist trade. We didn't go to church whilst we were there.

We returned home for the New Year and had to start work straight away, no time for jet lag. It was a particularly tough time at work for me in the print industry and Judy was the Nurse Manager running the Occupational Health departments for several local hospitals which was a very demanding position.

news summarised in thirteen words! I can't recall how many times I have shared those words when preaching or teaching on basic evangelism. Dr Osborn was a great encourager. He spoke to Kevin and me about the need for people to go out before the ministry to 'prepare the ground' for outreach events. This, he explained, was something his wife Daisy would do before he went anywhere to preach. They were truly an amazing team working to take God's message around the world and a great lesson in the need for teamwork.

I was now out every weekend doing street evangelism locally for the church which had started an outreach programme. Some weeks we would go into Stratford in East London and hold meetings in the town hall. Once a month we held a Sunday evening service in the church called 'Music and Miracles'. At these events the choir would sing, the gospel would be preached and people would be invited forward for prayer. It was wonderful to see God touching people's lives. The day before each event, a team of us would be in the locality handing out flyers and inviting people to come.

I remember one particular Saturday; we were doing street outreach in the nearby town of Epping. We had been there a while and the team members were coming up to me to say they'd finished their supply of leaflets. One of the team had other concerns:

'We've been looking for Judy and we can't find her anywhere! We've looked on both sides of the high street.'

I wasn't worried.

'What about the dress shops?'

'No, she's not in any of them, we looked through every window.'

'Did you go in?'

'No.'

I remembered Judy had liked a dress in the window of a shop called Glad Rags, so off I went. There she was, emerging from the fitting room, dress in hand, heading to the counter. Judy still had her leaflets and as she was paying the bill she said to the shop manager, 'I am in trouble with my husband; I have all of these leaflets left – can you put one in each bag for me?'

That Sunday evening a lady came to Music and Miracles. 'I found this leaflet in my carrier bag, that's why I came.'

Judy's leafleting technique vindicated!

Another person who came shared how he had found a discarded leaflet on a bus seat. God works in mysterious ways, there is no formula in reaching out and I have never forgotten this.

In June 1999 the ministry team took the whole choir on a nine-day missionary trip to Bulgaria, visiting seven cities. The hosts were Milcho and Annie Totev. Milcho was a Bulgarian Pastor with a very infectious character, a man who went out on the street to meet people. At our first location, the seaside town of Bourgas, Milcho called to me: 'Brother, let's go fishing!' We went out together 'fishing for souls'. As I spoke no Bulgarian, Milcho had brought along an interpreter. This was a new experience for me, having to rely on someone to translate what I wanted to say. Again this brought home to me the necessity for teamwork.

This mission trip gave me an insight into how the people had been suppressed by communism and the need to bring the good news of the gospel. It was an amazing time for both Judy and me being part of the choir. Looking out on those faces we saw many lives touched as people heard the good news. They were being released from the oppression that they had been living under. God was doing miracles of healing in every city we visited. God placed a desire to work in Eastern Europe in my heart.

Later that year Milcho and Annie paid a visit to the UK. Judy invited them to our home for dinner and our friendship grew. Then, typically, one day Milcho said, 'Come on, let's go fishing!' We took to the streets! This was the beginning of my links with Bulgaria.

> *"Come, follow me," Jesus said, "and I will send you out to fish for people."'* (Matthew 4:19 NIV)

Chapter 10

THE ALL CHURCHES MIRACLE CRUSADE TENT MISSION

AUGUST 1999

Dr T.L. Osborn was the inspiration behind the tent crusade. He was to be the main speaker and he wanted it to be an event that included all churches. Many local churches were involved in planning the event and we travelled far and wide promoting the tent crusade,

inviting church leaders and their congregations. Groups came from Belgium, Bulgaria and other parts of Eastern Europe as well as the UK.

The tent was pitched at Brizes Park just outside Brentwood. It was yellow-and-white candy striped and it glowed at night in the landscape – the light could be seen from the road. This gospel tent could hold 3,000 people.

In three simple steps Dr Osborn shared the heart of the gospel over three days:

- God is love
- Jesus came to show us God's love
- You can live the life of Jesus

There were spectacular miracles during this crusade. At the end of one meeting Dr Osborn said, 'I'm not going to call people out, but if you want prayer for healing, I want you to put your hand on the part of your body where you need a touch from God.' God doesn't need the touch of a man's hand to heal people (although he often uses that means). God is sovereign and when He does the work, it is done.

It was at the crusade that I first met Drs Kevin and Leslie McNulty. They had worked closely with Dr Osborn for many years and with him they had a vision to start a tent mission in Russia and across the former Soviet Union. They already had one tent which they used for crusades but their vision, called Tent 100, was to put 100 tents in the mission field. Kevin and Leslie had brought with them several evangelists from the Eastern European countries of Belarus, Russia and Ukraine who were all ready to go on to the mission field. As I learned more of how Kevin and Leslie had started with the first tent in Belarus, I became more intrigued by the work and eagerly listened to pearls of wisdom from these two experienced missionaries who themselves had learnt so much travelling in support of Osborn Ministries.

Travelling with the McNultys was a young man called Yauheni Hurovovich from Minsk in Belarus. Immediately we felt a kinship, something special between us in our passion for Jesus. From him I learnt a new word *Druk* which means 'friend'. He wanted me to go to Belarus and I promised that I would. We exchanged email addresses so that we could stay in touch.

Yauheni and I were both inspired by the teaching of Dr Osborn during this conference and what he said then has made a lasting impression on me for teaching evangelism. I have used and adapted Dr Osborn's teachings to make my own teaching presentations.

After the crusade was over Dr T.L. Osborn spoke again at our church and two things stand out in my memory from this time. Firstly, an appeal was made to support the vision of Tent 100 and a collection taken to raise money to buy a second tent. The money given was sufficient to buy two tents and to provide help with the infrastructure of the Tent 100 centre. Secondly, Dr Osborn had a special word of encouragement for the choir when he said, 'This is the most wonderful choir I have ever been around in my life, and I've been around a lot of choirs! Every song is a dynamic, powerful, miracle sermon!' It is so important that we choose the hymns and songs that we sing carefully because I know, from my own experience, that God can speak to us through the words that we sing.

I so wanted a chance to speak to Dr Osborn personally but the opportunity never came as he seemed to be whisked away at the end of the long meetings before I could get anywhere near him. On the Friday evening, as we were at home getting changed into our choir uniforms ready for the service, I said to Judy, 'I would really love to talk to Dr Osborn tonight, Judy.' And then I said, 'Oh God, I want to talk to Dr Osborn, to ask him how he started sharing the gospel.'

It was, once more, an amazing night of worship, teaching and prayer. Once he had finished ministering, Dr Osborn was once again whisked away. Disappointed, I thought to myself, 'Oh well, that's that.'

Judy and I had rushed home from work, stopping only to change into our choir robes, having no time to eat. 'Come on, Judy,' I said, 'let's go and get something to eat.' We ended up in a burger place in Brentwood just before closing time. We were reflecting on the service when we saw our friend Dave Rees knocking at the door. The door was locked and he wanted to be let in. It was late and we were their last customers. Judy persuaded the manager to open the door. In walked Dave and guess who was behind him – Dr T.L. Osborn. God had answered my prayer. I spent the next forty-five minutes talking directly with Dr Osborn. He was such a humble man, patient and encouraging as he shared with us. What an inspirational time! God always hears the desires of your heart. Especially a simple cry.

The Miracle Crusade was also the catalyst for a church plant in London by Milcho Totev and Dimitar Bouliev to serve the Bulgarian community. It's wonderful to see and be a small part of this fellowship as it continues to grow. It has been a lasting relationship for me both here and in Bulgaria.

I continue to see that God wants us to have a personal relationship with HIM!

'Jesus answered and said unto her, If thou knewest the gift of God, and who it is that saith to thee, Give me to drink; thou wouldest have asked of him, and he would have given thee living water.' (John 4:10)

'In that day you will no longer ask me anything. Very truly I tell you, my Father will give you whatever you ask in my name. Until now you have not asked for anything in my name. Ask and you will receive, and your joy will be complete.' (John 16:23–24 NIV)

Chapter 11

TALES OF THE UNEXPECTED BROUGHT A GREAT CHANGE

We received a call one Saturday morning saying, 'Have you heard about Michael Reid?' We knew that our pastor had been unwell as other people had been leading the services but what followed was the most shocking news. We were told he had admitted to having an adulterous affair. I couldn't believe it. I phoned my friend Simon who said, 'It's not a rumour, it's true.'

Judy and I wanted to see Bishop Reid and Ruth personally. Judy stopped off to buy some flowers for Ruth. We were invited into the house and I walked straight over to Bishop Reid asking him, 'Is it true what I have heard?' He said "yes" and that he was sorry.

'So you're not unwell now, but I understand why you feel ill,' I said. We were shocked like so many of the people who were now arriving at their house because, by now, the rumour had become public knowledge

Bishop Reid read a statement at a special meeting of the church in which he resigned from the board and stepped down from pastoral duties. He accepted responsibility for what he had done, apologised to his family and those whose trust he had betrayed and asked for forgiveness.

It's not for me to make judgements. A scripture came to me at the time: 'Let the one who has never sinned throw the first stone' (John 8:7 NLT).

I am so grateful to God for the way He used Pastor Reid to bring a gospel message that changed my life forever. I had seen God use him in a miraculous way with people being saved, healed and delivered from 1993 until 2008. His wife Ruth had been a great support to my first wife Eileen during her illness.

When I reflect back over this period, I realise that I learnt so much. Through this time I had been exposed to some amazing preachers, teachers and ministries. The opportunities I had to work with these ministries were an awesome experience. Seeing how different people worked in the kingdom of God was a valuable learning curve for me.

During this time the Oral Roberts satellite Bible college was established here in the UK. We spent three years doing a BA Practical Theology course. This was an American degree linked to one's previous qualifications. I am proud to say Judy has her full BA degree. I was not entitled to a BA degree but I did obtain a Diploma in Practical Theology.

I know nothing is ever wasted in the kingdom of God. The biggest lesson I learnt is: don't put your trust in man; we are all flesh and weak. God alone is Holy. 'It is better to trust in the LORD) than put confidence in man' (Psalm 118:8)

Now when I am unsure in any situation I say to myself, 'What would Jesus do?'

He would go to the Father and pray. Scriptures come to my remembrance:

'Trust in the LORD with all your heart and lean not on your own understanding. In all your ways acknowledge Him. And He shall direct your paths.' (Proverbs 3:5–6 NKJV)

'When the Spirit of truth comes, he will guide you into all truth. He will not speak on his own but will tell you what he has heard. He will tell you about the future.' (John16:13 NLT)

Chapter 12

NEW MINISTRY AND ROLE

The church had a new leader, albeit in a part-time capacity. He came to meet with me and Judy to talk about how the church could move forward. He asked me if I could look after the evangelism in the church. We both said we wanted to support the church going forward but we needed to pray for God's direction in what He was planning. I believed God was telling me to start a children's ministry for church members' children and reaching out in the community. I had already seen one model for this when I visited Metro Ministries during a trip to New York. What impressed me was the way Bill Wilson's ministry was training young people to become leaders who related so well to the children.

Judy used her gift of hospitality to invite people to our home for a meal which gave people a chance to talk and fellowship with the new pastor, Peter Linnecar, and his wife. It was during one of these lunches that a couple new to the church, Stef and Marie Thomas, crossed our path. Both were experienced in puppetry and children's ministry. I knew God had spoken and was now confirming it by bringing the right people together. He also gave me a name for this ministry.

Ark Bible Club was formed in October 2008 at my house. We had a great response from people wanting to be involved. I became Uncle Peter leading the ministry, along with Auntie Sue who was a schoolteacher. We had Auntie Dorothy, Marie's mum, who was gifted at writing dramas. Our aim was to share foundational biblical messages through stories and dramas. We wanted it to be fun, having a high-energy time with lively action songs that children

could sing and jump around to so they would be ready to listen to the messages we had prepared. This was something I gleaned from my visit to Metro Ministries.

We trained older teenagers to be leaders who in turn would train the younger generation to come into their own through lively worship. We gave them training as puppeteers. Working behind the curtain rather than standing directly in front of their audience gave even the shyest individuals the confidence to minister. We could see these young people growing as they too were having fun. My heart was to establish them as future leaders amongst the young people, something that had never been encouraged before. The aim was for them to have an identity, a sense of belonging to the work, so I had T-shirts made with the person's name on the back. This again followed the Metro Ministries' model. It was wonderful to see young people develop over the years. The young leaders owned Ark Bible Club. This brought tremendous fellowship amongst the young adults and brought fresh ideas for the children's activities.

Now, for the children, I wanted to instil a point of personal relationship, which comes through prayer. For me this had begun as a child with the Lord's Prayer. It has been the touchstone of my relationship with God and I am forever grateful. I was passionate about instilling this into children at a young age so that they knew they could have their own relationship with God, they didn't have to wait until they were grown up; it wasn't just a thing for parents. I had an A3-poster made of the Lord's Prayer; every child received a poster when they visited Ark Bible Club. The poster was very colourful with the Ark Bible Club logo and a rainbow just the same as on the front of the leaders' T-shirts. The children were so excited to receive these. They would come back and tell us that they'd put the poster up in their bedroom, how they were learning the Lord's Prayer with their parents and how they were looking forward to being able to say it themselves at Ark Bible Club. I loved to sit on the floor with all the children sitting around and pray the Lord's Prayer with them. It became a tradition to let a youngster who felt confident enough to use the microphone recite it to their friends. We also produced bookmarks with scriptures to tie up with our teachings so the children would go back and share with their parents. Recently I was shown an Ark Bible Club bookmark by someone who is still using her Lord's Prayer bookmark.

The talents of the young people were being given the opportunity to blossom as they planned the teaching programme and devised crafts and games to illustrate the message that they wanted to get across. The meetings always concluded with a puppet sketch which all ages found engaging. It was a good way to unite at the end of our time together as well as to underline the theme of the session. It was evident the model was working as the young leaders were building relationships with the children and with each other. As the team grew in confidence I was able to step back a little, which coincided with my increasing commitments abroad.

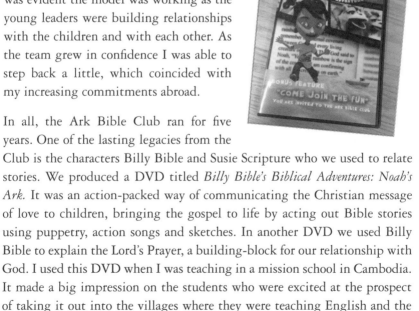

In all, the Ark Bible Club ran for five years. One of the lasting legacies from the Club is the characters Billy Bible and Susie Scripture who we used to relate stories. We produced a DVD titled *Billy Bible's Biblical Adventures: Noah's Ark*. It was an action-packed way of communicating the Christian message of love to children, bringing the gospel to life by acting out Bible stories using puppetry, action songs and sketches. In another DVD we used Billy Bible to explain the Lord's Prayer, a building-block for our relationship with God. I used this DVD when I was teaching in a mission school in Cambodia. It made a big impression on the students who were excited at the prospect of taking it out into the villages where they were teaching English and the Bible.

The DVD has proved to be a great outreach tool for children. The first time I used it was in the jungle in Malaysia. Nobody understood a word that was spoken but it was a real icebreaker. I have taken it with me on ministry trips around the world; I know there are copies in Bulgaria, Belarus, Malaysia, Russia, Singapore, Uganda and Zambia.

In 2009 we founded another ministry within my home church called JAM. 'Jesus and Me' was for teenagers, the idea being to give them time to fellowship together once a week. We held meetings in a marquee and brought in table-tennis tables (several of the youngsters were amazingly talented players) and we purchased pool, air hockey and indoor-football tables. The idea was to have a 'God slot' at the end of every evening and sit around discussing relevant issues over food. We would have film nights once a month. In the summer months we held barbecues.

We had quite a wide age group from 11–18 years old so it was not always easy to make discussions relevant to the whole group. We found that 'Christianity Explored' had just the programme we needed. One of the modules, 'Soul', was a great course with age-appropriate material that enabled us to split the age groups. We had almost sixty young people at one point.

The church was undergoing a change in structure under Peter Linnecar who had now been appointed as Senior Pastor in a full-time capacity. There was now to be a leadership team of six people who would actively support particular areas of the ministry going forward. I was surprised when I received a call asking me if I would accept a role in the team. My real passion was outreach and this was the aspect that I was asked to focus on in particular.

I was grateful for the way God had led me with the children and youth work, the experience proved invaluable on my missionary trips but I was praying for more opportunities. Needless to say, it didn't happen the way I expected.

Chapter 13

TALENTS AND GIFTS

I believe we all have abilities and talents. Sometimes they come naturally to us, sometimes we have to work at them. Some gifts God gives supernaturally. The greatest gift of all for me is to have the understanding of the love of God and knowing that God loves me.

One day, in my office at church, I found myself meditating upon the 'new commandments' of love that Jesus gave us.

> *"'Love the Lord your God with all your heart and with all your soul and with all your mind." This is the first and greatest commandment. And the second is like it: "Love your neighbour as yourself."'* (Matthew 22:37–39 NIV)

These two great commandments deal with loving God and others. This was challenging! How could I use the talents that God had given me to express this? I'd already been spending time talking to people and sharing God's love. I began to think about producing a tract with a message about LOVE. At school one of my best subjects (other than sport!) was art. This was a talent that God had given me that led me on to a career in design and printing.

I had bought myself a new MacBook and signed up for a course to learn how to use many of the applications on the Mac system. The one that really interested me was a creative package. I learnt how to operate this program which enabled me to produce my first tract. I found that the pictures, illustrations and text came together easily. The tract shows two young children with their arms over each other's shoulders with the word LOVE written in the sand, and on the inside the scripture from Mark's gospel entitled 'God's Footprint for Love'.

> *'Each of you should use whatever gift you have received to serve others, as faithful stewards of God's grace in its various forms. If anyone speaks, they should do so as one who speaks the very words of God. If anyone serves, they should do so with the strength God provides, so that in all things God may be praised through Jesus Christ. To him be the glory and the power for ever and ever. Amen.'* (1 Peter 4:10–11 NIV)

> *Your talent is God's gift to you. What you do with it is your gift back to God.* Leo Buscaglia

Seeing the tract finished and the way it was received was a great encouragement to continue to develop this route for putting the gospel message into people's hands. I produced my second tract with a signpost and a series of road signs with scripture and text appropriate to each sign, beginning with the STOP sign: 'Let's STOP and consider what direction we're heading in.' It has been a real blessing to see people read these tracts and an even greater blessing when we hear of a response.

You will have read throughout this book the value I place on the Lord's Prayer and communicating it to others; how my parents had influenced me through the prayer and how I wanted to do the same when I started a children's ministry. I was teaching a session on evangelism when a friend showed me a picture in a book of some hands and the Lord's Prayer. I thought, 'Wow! That would make an amazing tract.'

It certainly presented some challenging technical issues. First I went down the photographic route of producing the image of actual hands opening and closing, but this proved impossible. This is when other people's God-given talents and my professional skills came together. My niece Tessmin is a very talented artist. I was able to explain to her technically how the hand needed to fold together so the outer and the palms matched. She grasped what we were trying to achieve and produced a pen-and-ink illustration. Now I was able to take the illustration to Tony who had the skills to place the text I had chosen with the Lord's Prayer and finish the artwork to produce cut-out hands. The scripture opposite the prayer is:

Chapter 14

A PINT OF MILK AND MIRACLES
THAT FOLLOWED

We were on holiday in Malaysia in 2008 staying with Judy's brother Sunny. He invited me to go into the jungle with him and some members of his church. I didn't need any persuading, even with a 5 a.m. start. We met up with Bobby and his wife Fiona who, along with Sunny, had for some time been visiting an indigenous tribe called the Orang Asli. We set off in Bobby's big four-wheel drive vehicle which was loaded with gifts for the tribe and supplies for the trip, including some big jerry cans of water. It was a long journey from the capital Kuala Lumpur and during the drive I asked Bobby and Fiona about their previous visits to the tribes. They had been visiting faithfully for two years taking rice, tea, sugar and medication with them on each trip. It was interesting to hear how, on their initial trips, they had taken clothes and transported those in need of medical treatment to hospitals. Often they would take others with them to help.

Our final stop before going into the jungle was to buy some hot food and more supplies to take to the people. The abundance of loving-kindness was plain to see. As we were setting off again I was warned that we were now going off the main road through a plantation area and then we would be going off-road deep into the rainforest, following a bumpy track and coloured paint markings on trees. Then I asked the question, 'How have you been sharing the gospel with the people?'

The response I got was not what I was expecting: 'By meeting their needs.'

'Oh, oh, I see!'

Oh my God, oh my God, I said silently. *How am I going to communicate the gospel to these people?*

Well, I thought, *what would Jesus do? He would pray to the Father.* So that's exactly what I began to do. *Lord, please help me. How can I share with these people?*

Within minutes the Holy Spirit began to speak to me with a simple message. 'Take a bottle of milk!'

I remembered a teaching by Dr T.L. Osborn some years earlier about being a faithful, available, teachable, obedient, Spirit-filled servant.

'Stop! I need a bottle of milk,' I cried out. They all asked what I needed it for.

'I don't know; that's what God told me so I must get a bottle of milk.' We stopped and bought the milk.

 We entered the plantation, passed their security point and went on into the jungle. The track twisted and turned between the trees, gradually getting narrower and narrower. We were trying to spot the paint markings on the trees as Bobby carefully negotiated the car over the increasingly bumpy track. I was looking out for wildlife but didn't notice anything. Eventually we reached a sort of clearing from where we could see the village across the valley. Bobby decided to pull up and park and check the track ahead. He saw the headman in the distance and got out to talk to him. They were expecting us and the headman had come to guide us down the steep hill and across the valley into the village. Bobby said that if it had rained we would have got stuck using this route; as it was we were brushing the vegetation on both sides.

We eventually came to the clearing where the village was situated. The huts were made of sticks and leaves with old tarpaulins draped on top. The low huts were grouped close together and most had open fronts, something like pictures you'll see in *National Geographic* features on rainforest jungle.

Bobby asked me to sit in the car while he greeted everyone. He didn't think they had seen a white man before and he was telling them about me. When

I eventually got out of the car, the men became very nervous; they started calling out and pointing at me and then they disappeared into the jungle.

I was obviously frightening them. Bobby started to organise the unloading of the provisions and distribution of the food so I was left with the headman watching me from a distance, standing there with his stick of authority.

Eventually we were taken around the village; many huts had open fires in front of them. Finally we came to a hut where some women and young children were sitting on grass mats. It was a small group and I could see two teenage girls had their hands over their mouths, looking apprehensive. Bobby began by telling them about me, why I looked different and how I had come from that big bird in the sky – an aeroplane. Now it was over to me – and God of course. I think that God was already at work as the group was just women and children. I played the Ark Bible Club DVD featuring puppets and singing on my laptop. The group began to open up, they began to laugh and smile, which was such a relief to me.

Then I noticed something wriggling in a cloth hammock hanging from the hut ceiling. I called out to Sunny to take a look to see what was inside. I was thinking maybe it was a snake. You can imagine my surprise when Sunny called out, 'It's a bear cub!'

I was surprised but immediately knew why I had been told to buy the

bottle of milk! Ida, one of the Orang Asli ladies, stood up and took the bear cub from Sunny. I called out, 'Go and get the milk.' Ida began to feed the bear cub with the bottle of milk. God had this all planned! It was just the opportunity I needed to share the creation story and how God is our provider. I shared about all that we could see around us in the jungle: the sky, the trees and how the jungle provides them with food and animals all year round. I used how Ida was using the milk to feed the bear cub, how her milk breast-fed her children. Bobby was interpreting for me. I stopped to ask, 'Bobby, do they understand what I am saying?'

'Yes, they really understand. In this culture the girls are married and become mothers at a very young age.'

It was obviously God's plan to let my white face scare the men off!

One little girl had been crying on and off, and looked very uncomfortable. I asked Bobby to find out if any of them were unwell.

'Yes, this little girl, Leb, she has a skin disease. She's Ida's daughter. We have taken her to hospital before.'

We prayed for her. I put my hands together to pray. Fiona, Sunny and Bobby did the same. Bobby asked the group to copy us. I thought, 'What would Jesus do?' He would go to the Father and ask how to pray. So I did just that. I said the Lord's Prayer; Bobby translated after me and everyone else repeated it. I really felt the presence of God as we ministered. I believed God had done something special.

We were all excited. We packed up, said our goodbyes and left for the long drive home. We stopped on our way out of the jungle. Bobby, Fiona and Sunny were amazed at seeing the tribe putting their hands together to pray. They thought this was a sign and a breakthrough.

We didn't see a miracle while we were there; the marks were still on Leb's face when we left. However, on Bobby and Fiona's next visit two weeks later, Leb's skin was completely clear. The skin disease had gone! There were no marks on her face and body. It was a miraculous healing. This one little girl's miracle was to change the destiny of the tribe forever. I was so excited reading the news and seeing the evidence in the pictures Bobby sent to me.

Return to the Jungle

My next trip back to the jungle was in 2010. This time the men did not run away. As they saw me they pointed at me saying, 'Leb, Leb.' I did not frighten them. They helped us unload all the provisions and we sat around with them to eat a meal prepared from the food we brought with us. This time they were ready to hear and listen and receive the Word of God.

I knew exactly what God had laid on my heart and spirit to share: 'I am the light of the world.' How was I to share this with a group of people who had no concept of light other than daylight? They had no electricity; when the sun goes down they live in darkness with just the light of the cooking fires.

The first time God had laid on my spirit to bring milk; this time I was to bring 'light'.

I brought torches to show them light in the darkness. I began to share with them that it was possible for every one of them to have that light living within them.

Once again, the Holy Spirit really connected with them as I shared what Jesus did for us all on the cross. I was explaining to them that those who call on the name on Jesus would be saved.

Jesus would become their God and they would be His people. I asked them if they wanted God's light living inside of them as I shone the torch on each one. I asked them to make the sign of the cross across their own chest if they wanted to receive Jesus into their heart.

The Holy Spirit was giving me the words and actions as He led our gathering. It was amazing to see ten men making this commitment. God was not finished: a young man suffering from pain in his leg and stomach was healed, body, soul and spirit.

Some weeks later people were being baptised in the river. Bobby and Fiona were starting to see the fruit of their own and the churches' labour. God is so faithful. Now this amazing couple have brought water and electricity to the jungle – truly a miracle. Especially as I recall that we washed up-river and went to the toilet down-river!

Chapter 15

TURNED UPSIDE DOWN THEN 'OUT OF THE BLUE'

My life was being turned upside down. Things I had thought of as constants proved not to be:

Just after Easter in the church where I had become a born-again Christian, the pastor, a man whom I had trusted and respected, stepped down because of unseemly behaviour.

Work was becoming very uncertain: the economy was very volatile and I was travelling the length and breadth of the country trying to win business. It was hard for companies to get credit and the first thing they cut was their advertising. This put our company under extreme pressure to the point that it was no longer viable. The company went into receivership at the beginning of December and I was without a job.

For the first time in my life I was out of work. It was a tough time. I was mentally and physically exhausted. Fortunately, some months before, we had booked a holiday. It was due to start the day after I was made redundant. It seemed strange at the time, but looking back I can now see it was a blessing.

We came home for Christmas. Whilst we were away Judy and I had thought and talked about the future. This scripture kept running through my mind again and again:

> '*Trust in the* LORD *with all your heart, and lean not on your own understanding; in all your ways acknowledge Him, and He shall direct your paths.*' (Proverbs 3:5–6 NKJV)

I felt a peace and at rest. I had faith to believe that God was in control.

'Now faith is the substance of things hoped for, the evidence of things not seen.' (Hebrews 11:1)

It was January 2009 and I had to go to the Job Centre to register as unemployed. This was a humbling experience for me. I had been in full employment since the age of seventeen. At fifty-nine years of age I was told I didn't stand much chance of getting a job; senior positions were hard to find. I applied for jobs within charities; I was told I was over qualified.

Meanwhile, when I could, I was helping Judy on a voluntary basis with her medical screening company. I was also volunteering at the church: I had been appointed to the leadership team; I was developing the Youth and Children's ministries; I was helping out in many areas including media for the church and school. It was a strange experience, living by faith, not having a regular income. I had been considering – or rather dreaming – of working part-time in ministry whilst I was working but, to be truthful, having a mortgage and commitments always held me back.

I had been saying to Judy for a couple weeks: 'If only I could earn £25,000 a year I could sustain what I am doing now.'

That seemed an unrealistic hope as I was only getting £60 per week Jobseeker's Allowance and that was about to come to an end with no sign of a job. I had been to a couple of interviews but it was so obvious that as a print salesman I was expected to go after my old clients, which I couldn't do as my old company was trying to restart.

Out of the Blue

My mobile phone rang.

'Hello, Peter, I need to talk to you.'

It was one of my old clients from Ireland saying he wanted to meet me to talk about some work. My immediate response was, 'Where?'

'Hang on, Peter!' he replied.

'I am not ready to come and work in Ireland.'

82

'Hang on! I have a proposition I want to talk to you about. Will you meet me at Stansted Airport? I will explain more then.'

It was all very mysterious and I was intrigued. We met in the Radisson Hotel at the airport. First he ordered us both a big breakfast and then he said: 'I need your help and I will give you £25,000 if you agree to help me.'

You could have knocked me down with a feather! I couldn't believe what I was hearing. I immediately stopped eating to listen.

'I want you to find a buyer for my business,' he said.

'Why me?' I asked.

'I know I can trust you. I remember when you told me I was getting ripped off. You saved me a lot of money and I've never forgotten it.'

He carried on by saying, 'Take this folder; these are my accounts and business plans. You'll need to study them and then come over to Dublin to my offices. You'll receive a percentage of the sale of the business when you find a buyer. Meanwhile, I will put this gift straight into your bank account. If you find another job in the meantime that will be OK; I only need you to work a few days a month, let's say for the next year.'

On my way home, I was thinking it could only be God who had orchestrated this opportunity. When I told Judy she, like me, felt it was unbelievable. I looked through the accounts and quickly noticed what seemed to be some obvious and basic flaws. I showed the figures and projections to a friend who was a financial trouble-shooter working as an accountant in a big business. He agreed with my findings. I remember thinking 'nobody will buy this business'. If I was to earn any commission, immediate changes would have to be made to the business before I could even think about taking it to potential buyers.

Cutting a long story short, in total I ended up working less than a week on the project. I flew over to Dublin a couple of times and suggested some strategic changes. The business began to turn around over the first three months and was starting to make a profit. Now the owner suggested we waited another month to see how things went, and then another month, until he finally said, 'I don't want to sell up now.'

Judy was getting worried because I was literally doing nothing for him and living off this money.

'Are you sure he's not going to want the money back?'

'No, it really was a gift. He's happy that his business is now thriving,' I said.

The year was up. I phoned once more to check he still no longer wanted to sell his business. He didn't because it had completely turned around and was profitable.

It was nothing short of a miraculous provision!

Chapter 16

TURNED OVER

I had carried around a chapter from the Bible, Job 33, ever since I had my encounter with God back in 1993. I had asked so many people what it meant without receiving an answer that satisfied me.

For a long time, my Bible would continually fall open on this chapter, whatever copy of the Bible I opened. Certain verses would seem to jump off the page – especially the first eight verses.

Then one night I was lying in bed and I heard God speak to me in a dream, just like in Job 33. I woke Judy and told her what God had just told me to do. I knew I had to follow it. Judy listened and said, 'You'd better do what God has told you to do.'

God had told me I must contact the young Belarusian evangelist who I had met at the All Churches Miracle Crusade in 1999. I was to go to Belarus and pay for everything on the trip and go along with everything that Yauheni would have planned for me. I had not heard from Yauheni Hurovovich or tried to make contact with him for several years. We had become *druks* (friends) in 1999 and had both been inspired by the teachings of Dr T.L. Osborn. Yauheni had contacted me from time to time, inviting me to his home in Minsk, but for one reason or another I was never able to take up his offer. But I knew, even back then, God had plans for us. Now I began to send messages to the last email address I had for him and, a few weeks later, I heard back.

He was pleased that I had got in contact and when I explained the dream he readily agreed to arrange an outreach/teaching itinerary for me. I was excited at the prospect of meeting up with Yauheni again and to see what God had planned. We quickly fell back into the habit of calling each other *druk* when we spoke on the phone or sent emails. I was reflecting on the word 'friend' and thought of the nineteenth-century hymn 'What a Friend We Have in Jesus'. But we are more than friends with Jesus; we are Sons of God. As Sons of God we want to do His will and I believe that was the key to our close friendship: two people wanting to do God's will.

Money certainly wasn't a problem as God had already provided for me via the Irish businessman. I have learnt over the years that there are no coincidences. God has His purposes which are fulfilled in His timing. Now He was about to reveal the significance to my life of the scripture from Job that He had laid on my heart fifteen years previously.

It was now May and we planned for me to be in Belarus at the beginning of August. I had to apply for a visa at the embassy, which took several weeks to process. Finding a direct flight was difficult and the best option seemed to be to fly via Vienna with a two-hour stopover, and then to catch a connecting flight to Minsk.

When I arrived at Heathrow Airport there was thick fog and my flight was delayed. The flight attendants were telling us not to worry and that we would be taken directly to our connecting flights. At Vienna airport it was chaos; the place was full of disgruntled people who hadn't made their connecting flights. It was eventually suggested that I should fly back to Paris and get a plane to Minsk from there, to arrive later that evening. I arrived at the check-in desk to be told this flight had already gone. I asked about my luggage but nobody seemed to have a clue as to its whereabouts. I was then told I could not get a flight to Minsk until the next day. This meant an overnight stay in a hotel at Vienna airport. I eventually managed to contact Yauheni to explain that I would not be arriving that night but would be getting a flight the next day.

The next morning, before boarding my flight, I went to enquire again about my luggage. It was suggested that my bags were in transit from Paris and would be loaded directly onto the plane. We arrived in Minsk and I cleared through immigration and went to the luggage carousel waiting for my cases. Nothing arrived and I was getting frustrated trying to find out what was going on from people who only spoke Russian.

I called out, '*Druk, Druk,*' and eventually Yauheni appeared behind the security screen. He was able to explain that my luggage was lost and give the airport officials his home address where my bags should be sent when they finally arrived at Minsk airport. I learnt an important lesson: always put your Bible and ministry items in your hand luggage.

Yauheni had brought his wife Yulia and his two boys to meet me at the airport. We all headed back to Yauheni's small flat for coffee before going to the orthodox monastery where they had arranged for me to stay. The monastery was set in beautiful grounds and the apartment, where we sat down for our first meal together, was amazing.

It was easier when Yulia was around as she spoke better English than Yauheni. Yulia was concerned that I didn't have a change of clothes. She took my shirt away to wash and iron. Yauheni told me about the plans for the next day. 'We have a long drive tomorrow. You're going to share in my pastor friend's church and his son-in-law will interpret for you. He will have an English Bible that you can use.'

The next morning I shared a short testimony and gospel message. People came forward in response to my invitation for prayer. Yauheni told me later that the two ladies who responded had made a commitment to follow Jesus. The pastor and his wife took us to their home for dinner but on the way, we went to see the addiction centre that the pastor was running. It was a very moving and humbling experience. Local churches funded the centre and the facilities were basic. However, for some of the individuals this was the first time in their lives they had been shown love. Love shown in simple ways, such as the pastor picking up a table-tennis bat to join in the game. Everything had to be explained to me through the interpreter and any questions I asked had to be translated. I was learning to keep my conversations to the point, as everything took twice as long as usual.

Yulia was eager for us to be on our way back to Minsk so that she could take me to buy some clothes as I literally had what I was standing up in. We stopped at a supermarket where I could pick up what I needed: underwear, socks, toiletries and a spare shirt and T-shirt. Our next stop was to put fuel in the car and buy ice creams. I am sure it's a sign of a man who loves sharing 'Good News'. Like me, Yauheni can eat an ice cream at anytime!

The next day Yauheni and his family took me sightseeing around Minsk and then back to their flat as I had promised Yauheni Jnr and Timothy that I would play football with them. That evening I was going to share with a youth group and I was feeling a little frustrated as all the resources I had prepared were in my case which had still not arrived. Just as we were about to leave there was a knock at the door and someone was standing there with my case. Just in time! It brought a smile not only to my face but also to the two boys who were very happy to receive their Arsenal and Liverpool shirts. God is good!

At the youth group I was introduced to Olga who was to be my interpreter for the week. A local pastor, Irina, led the youth team and Olga explained that they were using the King's Kids model as the basis of their outreach. It was wonderful to witness their enthusiasm and to see how they took the Good News out. I shared a slide presentation of the children's and youth work I was doing in England. The next night I was back in the same building speaking to a church which had just come through a tough time, their former leader having run off with the church funds. The church was now being led by two lady pastors who had to restore the congregation's trust in one another and move the church on. God brought to my mind the prophetic word I had received from Benson Idahosa that I was to be 'an encourager all my life'. So, my message was that 'the enemy's biggest weapon is discouragement and he is the father of lies'. It brought smiles across everyone's faces. I then shared a short gospel message and two young ladies responded. As I left, the two pastors gave me a handful of bank notes saying they wanted to sow a seed into my ministry and thank me for coming to Belarus. It was so humbling. I asked them if I could sow the gift back into their ministry to help its growth. I have been back to Belarus to minister in that church and I've seen how God has caused their ministry to flourish.

The next thing Yauheni had arranged was a visit to an orphanage supported by local churches. It was a long drive but such a worthwhile and moving experience. The children were there for a variety of reasons: some because they had no parents, some because their parents were drug addicts, some because their mothers were single parents involved in prostitution. Many had suffered traumatic experiences. Whilst on the outside it looked very much like an institution, the children were trained in life skills so that they would be able to lead independent lives as adults. There was a needlework

and the Englishman. We both had to quickly change out of our jeans and into something a little more formal. The Bishop showed us around the diocesan facilities in the centre of the city that included a Bible college. He wanted to know what had brought a young Belarusian and the Englishman together.

It was an amazing first trip. I had felt the presence of the Holy Spirit as a fire burning inside every time I was ministering. God had opened so many doors and given me so many opportunities and it is fair to say the children at the orphanage had really tugged at my heartstrings. This trip was the beginning of the way God was to open up opportunities for Yauheni and me to work together and with others through the Tent 100 ministry.

Reflection:

God's timings are always right.

These are the words that came from my old King James Bible:

'In a dream, in a vision of the night, when deep sleep falleth upon men, in slumberings upon the bed; then he openeth the ears of men, and sealeth their instruction.' (Job 33:15–16)

GO

The desire to be in full-time ministry, sharing the Good News of the gospel, was now becoming a reality. 'Wow! God can do more than you can ask or think.'

'Now all glory to God, who is able, through his mighty power at work within us, to accomplish infinitely more than we might ask or think.' (Ephesians 3:20 NLT)

More opportunities to minister opened up: street evangelism, breakfast meetings, speaking at other churches and to children's and youth groups. I was able to give my testimony and share about the trips to the jungle in my local church, at community events and during interviews on Christian radio and TV. The connections I made would eventually open other doors and lead to more new experiences.

I met up with Avanti Ministries, a team of evangelists based in the UK. Every member of the group had so much enthusiasm and desire to proclaim the Good News of Jesus Christ. They came from diverse backgrounds: ex-football hooligans, involvement with the occult, time spent in prison, involvement in drugs, a soldier whose parachute failed to open. Each one of these men and women had an amazing story of how God had met them and transformed their life. Avanti had a fantastic training programme called 'Passion' which was designed to inspire churches to mobilise and help them in reaching out to their local communities. Connecting with a group of people who had a similar passion to my own was uplifting and I was delighted when I was invited to be part of the team.

I began learning how to share my testimony and give a gospel message effectively in three, five, ten or fifteen minutes. This a lot more difficult than having a twenty-five- or forty-minute spot as a main speaker. These training sessions could be great fun like the 'matchstick testimony' where you had to light a match and tell a story with a gospel message before the flame reached the end and burnt your fingers.

My first mission was to Grenoble and Lyon in France where I was given opportunities to share my testimony on several occasions. We were staying in the homes of people who were facilitating the outreach and I soon learned I wasn't the only one who snored! We would have really good fun and it turned out that most of the team were practical-jokers. One of the tracts we would use in the UK was a 'twenty pound note'. On one side it looked real but on the other it had a real challenging message. We would drop the tracts for people to pick up and read the 'Good News' or drop them into open shopping bags. Some of the more inventive ones amongst us would take the time to insert the tracts between the sheets of a roll of toilet paper, hoping someone would have a good read whilst sitting down!

This was one of the great things about being part of a ministry team: I was being exposed to creative ways of sharing the gospel through tracts and media. The saying 'iron sharpens iron' certainly proved to be true. Whilst most of the team was Essex based others came from further afield for our monthly get-together. We travelled around the UK wherever we were invited to share our testimonies as a means of sharing the gospel. It was really encouraging working with like-minded people.

The opportunity to travel abroad came when a team was being put together to go to Uganda. The team was made up of Tony (the founder of Avanti), John, George, Faye, Tina and me. It was an eye-opener to see the importance of teamwork. The Uganda mission emphasised to me the need for brothers and sisters around the world to work together in unity in order for the gospel to be preached to every person.

During the trip we went to Nakasongola Prison. This was my first visit to a prison and it was both daunting and amazing. Tony and John, who had been inmates themselves, and George, who was really experienced in prison ministry, spoke at the men's prison. Faye, Tina and I had the privilege of speaking in the women's prison. Many inmates gave their lives to Jesus at the meetings in both prisons. What touched me most were a few of the ladies who, with tears running down their faces, asked for a copy of the Bible.

On the Sunday morning I preached in a church in Kampala and I was given an opportunity to ask if anyone would provide a Bible for these women. One lady in the congregation jumped to her feet and rushed to the pulpit to offer her Bible. The Ugandan people we met were gentle and humble with a desperate need of spiritual and financial support. We witnessed an unbalanced distribution of wealth with some churches being very poor and others being prosperous, yet all had a heart for the gospel message to be preached to the nation. I was moved by the openness and hunger for the Word of God, as well as the desire to learn how to preach the gospel in their communities.

We took to the streets in Kampala where we saw many people saved. There was a real hunger amongst the people we encountered. The team ministered in eighteen different venues: at open-air crusades in cities, at schools for children whose parents had died of AIDS and pastors' meetings. We also held some teaching sessions on some modules of the Passion programme; time constraints meant that we could not cover all of the material. On one occasion we travelled right into the bush to hold a service for people who had literally walked miles to hear the gospel message we had to share.

In Uganda I was released into my calling to follow Christ and obey Him, becoming His messenger led by the Holy Spirit, to communicate the Good News of Jesus, to heal the broken-hearted and expand the kingdom of God. I was a captive to my calling as an evangelist. This is my passion to see people released in their God-given purpose. Matthew 28:19–20 reads:

> *'Therefore go and make disciples of all nations, baptising them in the name of the Father and the Son and the Holy Spirit. Teach these new disciples to obey all the commands I have given you. And be sure of this: I am with you always, even to the end of the age.'*

Wow! What an introduction to ministering in Africa and being part of a team. My eyes were being opened on a daily basis!

Later that year Yauheni invited me to serve with him in a Tent Ministry Crusade in Eastern Europe. I was to go to Vilnius in Lithuania to be part of an outreach with Yauheni and Eesuhuu Lypuhoeuy, the host pastor. It was a wonderful programme consisting of prayer and teaching seminars, street evangelism, a small gospel concert and an evangelistic message that incorporated a healing service each day.

Yauheni and his family were waiting to meet me as I cleared immigration at Vilnius airport. It was a lovely reunion with big smiles all round. We drove to the big tent pitched by the river in the middle of the city. It was a joy to hear Yauheni preach on the opening night and to see people respond.

We were staying in a flat that someone had loaned us for the week of the crusade. The next day started with a prayer meeting, followed by a seminar where I was to speak on evangelism to members of local churches and leaders from Tent 100. I used some of the Avanti Passion material entitled 'What is Evangelism' which had been translated into Lithuanian and Russian. They especially loved the practical side with tracts. The team left for the street in the city centre straight afterwards, very fired up for 'dropping the money tracts'!

The evening programme followed the same format each day, starting with praise and worship, then an evangelistic message followed by a healing service. Each evening we saw a few more people arriving as the Good News was being shared; the crusade was gaining momentum.

My second full day in Vilnius and I continued with the evangelism seminar. Then I was asked to do a children's ministry group where I used the story of 'The Good Artist' by John Place; it was a storyline and an illustration. The youngsters and the leaders really enjoyed the story and were challenged with Jesus being drawn coming to take away their stains to save them. Olga and Kirill, a couple who lived at the Tent 100 headquarters in Moscow, led the evening service. They sang and Olga played the violin, in fact she made it talk. Their little daughter Misha also joined in – an amazingly musically gifted family. Then they preached the gospel and once more people received Jesus, some received miraculous healings and others were delivered from drinking problems.

The next evening Olga and Kirill again led the worship but it was my turn to share the gospel message. By now word of the crusade had got around so the tent was quite full. I stood on the platform with my interpreter and gave my testimony of how God had changed my life. It needed to be short and to the point as speaking through an interpreter takes twice as long. I re-emphasised my testimony using the 'tear and share' illustration with a piece of paper. The paper is folded as you tell your story. Then you tear it and use the paper pieces to spell HELL, then rearrange the pieces to spell LOVE. I could hear gasps in the audience as I shared  and revealed the CROSS, asking people to stand to their feet and come to the platform. A great number responded and came forward quickly. To be honest the rush took me by surprise. I had shared this message before but this time it made a real impact. The atmosphere in the tent was awe-inspiring.

Yauheni joined me on the platform and began praying for healing. More and more people continued to join us at the front. It was wonderful hearing the testimonies from those who came forward, of those lives that had been touched: body, soul and spirit.

Oh my God, what a marvellous week. We felt the love of Jesus in the unity of the team drawn from many nations coming together to proclaim the Good News. We saw the love of Jesus in the many lives that were transformed. We witnessed the power of God at work!

Yauheni said to me, 'You've seen what happens in a tent. We need to do a tent mission together in England.'

His face was beaming as he challenged me. He took me to the airport and his parting words were: 'I'll look forward to coming into England again, and we need to do a tent mission!'

Pastor Peter Linnecar met me at Luton Airport and I was still so excited by the things I had witnessed in Vilnius that I spent the entire journey home telling him what had happened in the tent. I finished by saying, 'We need to pray for God to confirm if He wants us to do a tent mission here in England.'

Chapter 18

BEGINNING OF THE WAY

I had returned from Lithuania really challenged by what I had seen. I was excited by what I had been a part of with Yauheni and the rest of the Tent 100 team. I really prayed for God to guide me as to how I could bring a tent mission to England. I believed God was telling me it wasn't just for my home church but an event for all the local churches to participate in. I shared this with my home church leadership and asked if I could present the idea to the local group of churches.

Then, at the next church leadership meeting, God spoke to the situation. Revd Canon George Kovoor joined the leaders each month to chair the meeting and provide oversight. He said:

'I have come with a Word for you all. These verses are from Isaiah 54: *'Enlarge the place of your tent'* and *'Don't let any weapon stand against you.'* Does this make sense to any or all of you!'

Wow! God had answered and confirmed the way forward so clearly to me and the leaders.

I was then given the green light to approach other churches in the town.

Now I had to find a big tent. Our church had sold their big marquee but the chairman of trustees, Terry Pearce, put me in touch with the new owner, a tent evangelist called Tim Grant whose ministry Spearhead is based in Hampshire. Terry had a good relationship with Tim and had helped him put up the tent on several occasions. I had a brief conversation with Tim explaining the vision to bring a tent mission to Brentwood. Tim came up to Brentwood to meet me and discuss the idea in more detail. He was enthusiastic and encouraging and it was the beginning of a friendship that was to see us travelling together.

I continued to pray about this event. God once more gave me a word from scriptures, Acts 9:2: 'People of the way'; followers!

I searched the Bible for other references to 'the way'.

Jesus taught about two ways which are recorded in Matthew 7:13–14: the broad way that leads to destruction and the narrow way that leads to life. Jesus also claimed to *be* the way (John 14:16):

a. The way to truth and life.

b. The only way to the Father.

It seems likely that Jesus' statements led to the use of 'The Way' in the Book of Acts.

Now we had a name for the crusade it was time to take the vision to the BADEF (Brentwood and District Evangelical Fellowship) church leaders. I shared with them how Yauheni had the vision to partner with me in bringing a tent mission to England, how he had invited me to Lithuania to see for myself the effectiveness of tent missions, how he had shown the principle of networking, bringing churches together to hold an 'outreach festival'. I couldn't take the local leaders to Lithuania to see what I had seen but I could bring Yauheni to England to share the gospel.

We had a few hurdles to jump over such as preaching the gospel through an interpreter. 'I am not sure this will work,' one minister said. It was frustrating, to say the least. I could only politely respond, 'What about the Holy Spirit?'

Miracles, some ministers believed, only happened when Jesus walked the earth.

Another said, 'I think holding tent missions is a bit old fashioned.'

I had seen God move in tents. I had seen people getting healed and saved even when the message and the prayer were delivered through an interpreter. It wasn't easy to overcome the leaders' reservations, but God had given us a

Word: 'Enlarge the place of your tent' – 'Don't let any weapon stand against you!'

Eventually it was agreed to delay The Way Festival for a year to summer 2013. Yauheni was to come over in 2012 to preach and share the vision. We met with Tim Grant to decide on a site. We wanted a neutral site to bring the public and churches together. It was important to have unity, with as many churches as possible partnering with the event both physically and financially. All the possible sites we looked at in the town had issues with security, logistics or costs. We eventually decided to use the church grounds because we had none of these issues.

Thankfully, after Yauheni came over with Vitali his interpreter, a few ministers were inspired to get behind the vision. In the forefront were Alan Cass, Jem Trehern, Gary Seithel and Peter Linnecar from my home church. We set up a steering group with the BADEF chairman and set the date for The Way Festival the following summer.

It was a frustrating time organising this event. Several years later I have seen tent missions in Europe facing opposition, sometimes in the middle of the event. Nowadays I don't mind a bit of opposition. In fact, whilst it can be frustrating, it is encouraging at the same time. History shows us that when the gospel is preached, opposition comes along; Jesus himself had enough opposition, didn't He?

Chapter 19

CONNECTING IN MOSCOW

Opportunities began to open up. Yauheni wanted me to join the 2012 conference for the Tent 100 evangelists held in Moscow. It was an annual event hosted by Kevin and Leslie McNulty for the entire team of tent evangelists across Eurasia and Bulgaria.

I travelled alone to Moscow and at the airport looked expectantly for a signboard with my name on it. After an hour I was still waiting for somebody to appear. I didn't have the address of where I was going. I had no contact phone number other than Yauheni who I knew was driving from Minsk in Belarus to Moscow.

I seemed to be the only person from the flight left in the arrivals hall so eventually I decided to call Yauheni. I had to leave a message but he finally called me back to say a driver was on his way to collect me and an American whose flight had been delayed. I was so relieved when a young man arrived some two hours later with a signboard bearing my name. I was thirsty and busting to go to the toilet!

The event was held in the Tent 100 headquarters on the outskirts of Moscow. On the ground floor a tent-manufacturing centre had been set up; the other floors were used as dormitories for many of the visiting evangelists. I was booked in down the road at a guesthouse with some other evangelists from Russia, Ukraine and other parts of the former Soviet Union.

I soon became friends with Andre from Krasnodar. He spoke good English and through him I connected to more people. We would pool our food together for breakfast everyday and 'make new friends'. We laughed a lot and had such a good time. We slept three or four in a room and it was pretty cold, so cold in fact that the plumbing froze and we had no hot water to shower. The two-mile walk to the mission centre through the snow certainly woke us up in the mornings.

The conference began each morning with a time of worship followed by a time of introduction and sharing before Leslie and Kevin would teach, bringing challenging and inspiring messages. There were three 45-minute sessions before lunch and another three sessions in the afternoon. It was such an encouragement to hear from the many evangelists who held tent missions throughout Eurasia.

Everyone had such a passion for reaching the lost. Every day a different person would be given time to share what he or she had been doing in their country. What I had seen in Lithuania was happening in so many places. This to me was the gospel; the Good News was preached and signs and wonders followed. I was hearing testimonies of amazing miracles of healing and salvation. I had arrived in Moscow knowing only Yauheni and some of the team from Belarus, the musicians Kirill and Olga and, of course, Leslie and Kevin, but as the conference gathered momentum I was getting to know more and more people.

Listening to Kevin and Leslie was just like being with Dr T.L. Osborn; they were so passionate about their calling and so encouraging to others. I had an opportunity to talk with them during one of the meal breaks. They knew about the discouraging times I had gone through in my home church. Kevin said: 'I want to pray with you. I believe you will see God use you, and signs and wonders will follow you wherever you go.' Kevin also said he would get Dr Osborn to write to me.

It was as if Kevin's prayer swept away previous disappointments and frustrations. The conference ended with a 'team time' with people unveiling their plans for the year ahead in different cities and countries. I received invitations to join evangelists in various countries and to lead teaching sessions at mission schools that were planned. I knew God was revealing a new way forward in my journey.

I really felt 'ignited', full of fire within me, full of the Holy Spirit. 'A hot wire connection!' I went out on the street near the mission centre with a couple of guys from the conference. I took some dollar tracts and used these to share the gospel with some Russian folk who were waiting for a bus. One of the Russians could understand most of what I was sharing and my friends from the centre translated for the others. The smiles of joy on the faces of the two people who accepted Jesus into their lives set our hearts rejoicing too. We all had a real buzz for the rest of the day as we went back to the conference.

The conference time was like a new beginning for me. I no longer felt restricted. I felt so connected.

I returned from Moscow with my expectations having taken a giant step forward. This was bolstered further when about two months later I received a letter from Dr Osborn. It was the most inspiring of letters telling me how thrilled he was that Yauheni was planning a crusade in England and encouraging me to get involved with the Tent 100 work. The letter was so personal that Kevin had obviously told Dr Osborn of all the frustrations and setbacks that I had gone through. One scripture in particular really spoke to me:

> *'But we all, with unveiled face, beholding as in a mirror the glory of the Lord, are being transformed into the same image from glory to glory, just as by the Spirit of the Lord.'* (2 Corinthians 3:18 NKJV)

This scripture spoke in the same way as the time I heard that inspirational message from Dr Osborn in England in 1999, summed up in the song 'You're the Only Jesus Some Will Ever See'.

July 2, 2012

Dear Brother Peter Ruck

'We Christians are mirrors that briefly reflect the glory of the Lord. And as the Spirit of the Lord works within us, we become more and more like Him.' 2 Cor 3:18 LB

It was a great pleasure to receive your wonderful letter and report of various Ministry outreaches in which you are involved. It is so wonderful to commit yourself to work with people who want to reach the unreached and love the unloved. Our world is in such need of His love so I know God is going to richly bless your life.

I am so glad to hear of your work with Avanti Ministries, the organization focused on teaching the lost and preaching the Gospel. I hope your Mission to Zambia materializes because as you reach into the prisons and hold outreaches in Zambia you will help change that nation. Thank you for the kind words that you spoke about me influencing others so the seed of the Gospel continues to spread everywhere. One hundred years after we are gone from this world, the seed that we have sown will continue to proliferate with the message of Christ. Since I saw you we have had a marvellous time of ministry in the south of India where the need for the Gospel is so desperate and where people are so responsive.

I am glad that you follow some of the postings on facebook and I trust that they will be a blessing. I am glad to hear that you have been ministering with the McNultys. They are a wonderful couple and are doing God's number one job of reaching the unreached throughout Russia and other nations. It is wonderful that you are being influenced by them.

May He bless you richly and may your dreams of reaching the unreached be manifested wherever you go as you proclaim the Gospel of Jesus Christ to the hurting people in so many areas where they are forgotten. They are lonely and are in need of spiritual help.

I close with my love to you and gratefulness to God for the way He has led you and will lead you into a great, successful time of reaching the unreached.

Your special friend in the Gospel

TL Osborn

104

hundreds of inmates receive Christ. We were not allowed to take our cameras or phones inside the prisons; we didn't need them because we could never forget what we saw.

In addition to the prison ministry we led evangelism training which was a real eye opener and an encouragement to the local pastors. We went into schools and hospitals and prayed for those in need. We worked very effectively in the towns and markets as, being four white men, we stood out in the crowd. 'Mzunga' they called us but what attracted them more than the colour of our skin was that they saw people being healed, giving their lives to Christ and being touched, body, soul and spirit.

In one town a Muslim man came looking for us. He told us that he'd had a dream and he wanted us to pray with him. George and I shared the gospel with him sitting on the wall in the centre of Chingola. Jehovah's Witnesses approached us willing to listen to what we had to say. We shared from John 14:6 where Jesus said, 'I am the way, the truth, and the life: no man cometh unto the Father, but by me', and then I opened my Bible so that they could read the whole chapter. We worked in pairs: normally John and Shaun went together and George and I would wander off in a different direction. As we were walking through a market area we got into a conversation with a young girl called Constance. She was sweating and looked quite unwell. She told me she was an orphan being brought up by an aunt and that she had malaria. We talked for a bit and I told her very simply, 'Jesus loves you and wants to heal you.' She looked surprised. I asked if she had a Bible and when she told me she hadn't I said I would buy her one. George jumped in with 'You can have mine!' We both prayed with her and then moved on talking to other people in the market.

The next day we were due to minister in schools: primary schools in the morning and secondary schools in the afternoon. After the morning session we went into town for lunch to a pie shop. I ate a steak and pepper pie but it didn't agree with me. I was so unwell that Sam, who was taking care of us, had to take me back to the Campbell's mission house where we were staying so that I could get some medicine and lie down for a while.

I was still dozing a few hours later when George, with whom I was sharing the room, came bursting in, full of excitement:

'Peter, wake up! Guess what, we shared with one thousand five hundred kids!'

This woke me up.

'Who do you think responded?'

He told me that Constance had come to the front and given her heart to the Lord and that she was totally healed of malaria. The medicine had worked for me. I was feeling better, especially after the news of Constance.

On Sunday morning we went out into the townships outside the central area of the city to preach in different churches. During our travels we spotted a large car park which had a massive wall painted white, ideal for a cinema screen. We had a projector and decided to show the *Good Artist* DVD. We connected the projector to a generator and soon a crowd gathered to watch the show. The message had a big impact and we were surrounded by people responding to the gospel as we ministered to them. We left Zambia praising God, knowing thousands had heard the gospel.

This was the year of the Olympics which provided many opportunities to share the gospel in London. A group from Avanti also went to open-air outreaches in Blackpool, first with Jenny and Keith Raby on the promenade under Blackpool's famous lights and later in the year for Music in the Park, which was another great weekend.

My last mission trip with Avanti was to the Scottish Border towns where some young American evangelists joined us. We spoke at various venues and were blessed to have Erik and Stephanie Rostad open each service by leading us in worship. They are a wonderfully gifted duo with Stephanie singing and Erik accompanying her on the guitar or violin. I have kept in contact with them over the years and in fact Erik designed the www.zealoutreachministries.co.uk website.

I had experienced so much and learnt so much during my time with Avanti Ministries but now I felt that God was calling me back to Russia and Eastern Europe and the Tent 100 outreach ministries.

Chapter 21

COMING FROM THE WEST TO THE EAST

I was going east to Russia to the Tent 100 conference for the second time. I had asked Tim Grant, an experienced UK-based tent evangelist, to accompany me.

Sometimes, with the benefit of hindsight, you can see how God brings people together with every detail carefully in place, like a spider's web. God brought Yauheni and me back together with the vision for a tent mission in England. I needed a tent and that established a connection with Tim, the new owner of the tent which had housed the All Churches Miracle Crusade. The crusade when Kevin, Leslie and Dr T.L. Osborn shared their vision and Tent 100 was launched.

I had been so inspired by the previous Tent 100 conference and I wanted Tim to meet everyone. I was excited at the prospect of spending more time with these like-minded people whose passion was to reach lost souls and to see people saved, healed and delivered; to have the opportunity to learn during the practical seminars from their experiences of running tent missions. It was a thrill to visit Red Square again with Sofi from Bulgaria, Yauheni from Belarus and Johannes from Estonia.

At the end of the conference Tim and I were invited to join Yauheni and Sofi to lead a four-day national evangelical seminar in Kumanova, the second largest city in Macedonia. An invitation we were delighted to accept.

So a few months later we were off again. I had a 4.00 a.m. start from Brentwood to Gatwick Airport where I met Tim to catch a flight bound for

Bulgaria. We were met at Sofia airport by Tim's interpreter. She drove us over the border into Macedonia to Kumanova where the conference was being held in a newly built church. It was a five-hour drive but a good opportunity for Tim to catch up with developments in the Bulgarian outreach.

Yauheni and Sofi spoke on the opening night of the conference. The delegates were pastors and church leaders from most of the Macedonian evangelical churches.

On Friday Tim and I spoke at the evening session. Saturday was an all-day event with three speakers in the morning: Phillip a young evangelist from Macedonia, Johannes a tent evangelist and Yauheni who was leading the conference. It was very well attended as even more delegates arrived from further afield, many travelling long distances to join with the local church leaders. In the afternoon teams went out to do street evangelism in the city in the freezing cold and it was a relief to be back indoors in the warm for the evening presentations.

Johannes started the evening followed by Tim's inspirational message which he finished with a practical illustration of leading people to Christ. I shared about the power of personal testimony, using an example from my own life and visually illustrating it with 'tear and share'. This is a firm favourite of mine, you can share it anywhere; one simple piece of paper can bring a real focus to your story and, more importantly, it centres people's attention on the cross. I also shared various ways of using the money tracts which caused a good deal of laughter.

The local pastors and ministries were so inspired they asked the team to return and speak at a tent mission the following summer. We were all surprised to hear them say they already had a tent! For the team it was a time of real bonding but at 'lights out' in the men's dormitory you needed to get your head down on your pillow real quick to grab some sleep before the snoring convention started!

Sunday morning we were all up bright and early. Members of the team were sent to different churches. I, with Evangelist Philip as my interpreter, was sent to Veles which was a two-hour drive from Kumanova. I counted myself lucky as we were able to enjoy a glimpse of Macedonia during the trip. Pastor Dragan and his wife Bilajana greeted us. It was a small church and he immediately began to apologise because many of the congregation were away as it was a national festival. Pastor Dragan had specifically asked that I be sent to his church as he was interested in puppet ministry. He was keen to learn about my involvement in the children's ministry in my own church and delighted to receive the *Billy Bible's Biblical Adventures: Noah's Ark* DVD. God always has a very definite purpose when He sends you somewhere.

Phillip, who had been paying very close attention to my 'tear and share' method at Saturday's seminar, was keen to share it himself with his home church. He then translated for me as I was preaching. As usual, at the end of a service I invited anyone who wanted to give their life to Jesus to come to the front of the church and I would pray for them. I didn't see anyone respond but I had really felt God was speaking to people through the message. As I prayed for the whole church I felt someone was too shy to respond but there was nothing that I could do about it.

As we were walking down the steps out of the church a man grabbed hold of my arm. He said that God had been speaking to him when I was preaching. 'I should have responded inside the church,' he said. 'Is it too late now? I can't stop shaking inside.'

'What's your name?'

'Dima'

'Well, Dima, the Bible says that those who call on the name of Jesus will be saved. Welcome, Dima!'

As I prayed with him to receive Jesus as his Lord and Saviour his face began to lift. Dima, who spoke excellent English, then said, 'I have such pain in my body. I have cancer. Will you pray for me?' I prayed for him again.

'I am still shaking, but the pain is a little better now.' He was now smiling. I called to Pastor Dragan and his wife to join us and they continued to pray with him. It reminded me that God sees our hearts and gives everyone the opportunity to respond to His love as He so wants to meet our needs.

There was time for a quick lunch, a request for me to return in the summer and a warm farewell before we set off on the long journey to Kyustendil in Bulgaria where we were to meet up with Tim to take the evening service in a Romany church. This was my first experience of a gypsy community but Tim was very experienced working with the Romany people through his tent ministry. It was a very lively church with a very passionate pastor. The seating arrangement was new to me: men on one side, women on the other, children at the back. Tim led the preaching and I just followed his lead, we both prayed for the sick. After the service one family we had prayed for came up and wanted their pictures taken with us as they were so excited that non-Romany people would come to share the love of Jesus with them.

It had been a long but rewarding day and now we had to drive back to our hotel in Bankya just outside Sofia. It seemed our heads had hardly touched the pillow before it was Monday morning and we had to be up and heading off to Plovdiv for Tim to meet up with several converts from his previous tent missions. Tim's friend Martin joined us for the journey and I learnt a lot just listening to them talk about the culture of the Romany people. God had really laid these people on Martin's heart and he was trying to relieve their poverty by helping them set up agricultural and small business projects. It was certainly a real eye opener for me to see so many people living in one room!

Then it was a two-hour drive back to Sofia to meet up with my friends Annie, Borislava (Buba) and Valdo. It was a very precious time as it was the first time Annie and I had met since Milcho's promotion to glory two years previously. We had a wonderful reunion meal in Bankya where Valdo and Buba were keen to share developments in the church since they had taken over as pastors.

Tuesday morning and another early start as we headed into Sofia for a pastors' breakfast and prayer meeting. This was a wonderful opportunity to have fellowship with around fifteen church leaders from the city and to build relationships. Then Tim and I were off to our second meeting of the day at a city shopping mall. Here we met with Sofi and Yauheni to review the Macedonian evangelism conference and compare notes on the ministry in Bulgaria and Macedonia. God had been so faithful; the gospel had been preached and signs and wonders had followed. We were also planning for the future: first a preaching and teaching mission in Belarus, then a trip to Moscow for Tent 100, and then back to Macedonia to hold a tent mission in July with possibly a return visit to Bulgaria.

That evening Tim and I were due to preach at the International Christian Life Centre in Lulin on the outskirts of Sofia at a prayer and outreach meeting. This was the church that Milcho and Annie had founded and it was good to be ministering with old friends Pastors Valdo and Borislava. I was looking forward to sharing my message – 'The Cross is our Passport to Heaven'. Tim preached after me and we both felt the presence of God as many responded to the message of salvation and healing through God's power. It was lovely to hear the testimonies from this evening and it was a wonderful ending to the mission to Macedonia and Bulgaria.

This was our last night in Bulgaria. Tim, Martin and their interpreter were leaving for Plovdiv early the next day before going on to Serbia so we said our farewells that night. In the morning Borislava came to fetch me and take me to see her parents' house where her father had started his first church in the back garden. Annie preaches there every Thursday and Sunday morning – a real woman of faith. A quiet interlude before I had to leave for the airport.

> '*Go into all the world and preach the gospel to every creature . . . they will lay hands on the sick, and they will recover.*' (Mark 16:15–18 NKJV)

After we returned to the UK I received the following testimonies from Pastors Vladimir and Borislava via email:

> 'We had two guest evangelists from England who were on a missionary trip to Macedonia and Bulgaria, they attended as guests of the monthly pastors' breakfast. The same evening the evangelists gave their testimonies. At the end of the service a prayer line for healing was formed, prayers started, Praise God. We experienced many miracles that evening. Here are some of them. One young boy he had for 4 years nails in the feet. A few

months ago he had an operation and they removed the nails, but the left leg grew shorter by more than 1 inch. After prayer Tim laid hands on him and his leg grew and became like the other one. A lady with "curtains" of the eyes received healing with totally clean eyes as Peter laid hands on her. They continued praying and another lady was feeling "ants" all over her body, following prayer this disappeared; her 16-year-old daughter who had only just started coming to church was touched. A young lady with a stomach disease was totally healed with no more pains. We are so thankful to God and wanted to share this with you both.'

Chapter 22

'TIME TO GO' MISSION SCHOOL

Yauheni had invited Tim and me to Belarus to teach on evangelism in a mission school. It was Tim's first trip to Belarus. We arrived in Minsk and were taken to lunch at a former communist eating house (canteen) where they served very traditional, and very good, food. In the afternoon we taught at a Bible school in the centre of the city.

The next day the mission school commenced with students coming from Belarus, Ukraine, Bulgaria and Russia. Tim and I had two sessions each to teach on evangelism during the day and Yauheni would arrive to do an evening session. The school was held in a respite centre for children who, during the week, lived in an orphanage. Each weekend would see

around twenty youngsters arriving from the orphanage and they would join us for breakfast. One morning we had been going through the 'tear and share' paper routine and I noticed two teenage girls who had been watching us intently but saying nothing. I smiled at them and they smiled back and then I realised they were both deaf. I decided to go through the tearing sequence again with both of them – doing my best to convey the message with the help of some of the other students. I finished by giving each girl the cross to keep.

The next weekend we were sitting down having breakfast when the matron from the orphanage walked over to the table asking who had been talking to her girls? All eyes looked at me. I wracked my brains to figure out what I could have done wrong. The matron told us how, through sign language,

the girls had shared with her about Jesus and the cross, and that the paper crosses had been put up in their rooms in the orphanage. My serious face changed immediately to a smile – I was not in trouble!

Sunday morning and Yauheni had arranged for me and Tim to minister in two different churches. Tim was collected and taken to a church that I had ministered in on my first visit to Belarus. Dima, our interpreter who was a Belarusian but lived America and had come to the mission school just to interpret, stayed with me and we waited from someone from the other church to come and collect us. This turned out to be a Sunday morning that I will never forget as long as I live.

We were ministering in a family church packed with people of all ages. Dima explained that many of the children went straight to Sunday school which was held in an adjoining room. The service began like any other with a time of worship, announcements and introductions, and then it was time for the preaching. I began by sharing my testimony followed by the gospel message. The words of knowledge flowed as people began to respond. There was a tremendous sense of freedom in the air.

People came forward for salvation as the Holy Spirit was touching people. They were being set free of pain and regaining movement in their limbs. It was a tremendous time of healing and liberation. 'Come to me, all you who are weary and burdened, and I will give you rest' (Matthew11:28 NIV).

Then came a moment that triggered a release of compassion like I have never experienced before. A young boy came forward. He appeared to be disturbed and very agitated. A carer followed him and sat on a chair in the front row. I looked down from the platform and smiled at the boy. I felt led to sit on the floor and invited him to join me. Dima immediately copied me and the three of us sat on the floor together.

My Spirit was filled with these words of Jesus: 'Let the little children come to me, and do not hinder them, for the kingdom of heaven belongs to such as these' (Matthew 19:14).

The boy calmed down and smiled back at me. I asked him to copy me by putting my two hands together and we prayed the Lord's Prayer together. Dima spoke to him and he copied my every movement. He became completely calm as we sat on the floor. People were sitting on the edge of their chairs in anticipation to see what God was going to do next.

What happened next was that parents and Sunday school teachers were bringing young boys and girls forward for prayer. We continued sitting on the floor surrounded by children, praying for each of them, knowing God was telling us to take our time with each child and their parents. I will never forget those eyes looking up at me and the miracles God did touching so many of their lives. There was such a presence of God as the anointing flowed through us. It's hard to express in my own words but 2 Corinthians 4:5–8 became a reality.

> *'For what we preach are not ourselves, but Jesus Christ as Lord, and ourselves as your servants for Jesus' sake. For God, who said, "Let light shine out of darkness," made his light shine in our hearts to give us the light of the knowledge of God's glory displayed in the face of Christ. But we have this treasure in jars of clay to show that this all-surpassing power is from God and not from us. We are hard pressed on every side, but not crushed; perplexed, but not in despair.'*

I recently contacted Dima to ask how he remembered that service: 'I remember it was a service filled with the sweet presence of the Lord. Parents, grandparents, Sunday school kids and teachers were so moved by the testimony you gave, they were moved to have you pray for as many sick people as possible.' He added that he believed that that whole area, just like most of the country, has many children who have been affected by the Chernobyl nuclear power station disaster. Eighty per cent of the fallout in the weeks following the explosion on 26th April 1986 was in the south of Belarusia, and it made around twenty per cent of the Belarusian land unusable for agriculture.

We went back to the mission school for two more days with the students. We had built a great relationship with this group and it was a rewarding time for

the students and mentors alike. Now, years later, it's good to read how these one-time students have flourishing ministries. This was the first 'Time to GO' mission school but since then there have been many others in different countries.

At the school God had one really special gift for me. Early in the week I noticed one young man in the group looking at me intently. He reminded me of the seventeen-year-old orphan I had met on my first trip to Belarus, the talented young carpenter who was about to leave the orphanage to make his own way in the world. I had continued to pray for Sasha over the years and now here he was learning how to share his faith. I think we both stared at each other in disbelief without saying anything. Then I just had to ask him, 'Were you brought up in an orphanage?'

'Yes. Do you remember me?'

Did I remember him?! Once more God was witnessing to us, to me, that He answers prayers and that we serve a faithful God.

On our final night Tim and I were sharing to a group in a large auditorium. We were both given words of knowledge and this brought a large response and many people came forward. It was getting late and we needed to draw the service to a close but there were so many people wanting prayer. Tim told me to raise my arms and we formed an arch. As people passed under the arch we prayed for each one. So many people were touched mind, body and soul that evening as the Holy Spirit ministered through us. This, to me, was a new way of praying for people, but God was present and the same anointing flowed. This became really apparent when a young man passed by me through the arch. He started to become very agitated, distressed and disturbed. Frankly, I had never seen anything quite like it. Tim got me to step back and asked the many concerned relatives to move away. Tim then rebuked the spirit and the man calmed down and became rational.

It was such a confirmation of God's faithfulness to be greeted by two young women whom God touched on my first trip to Belarus. As a travelling evangelist you usually only meet people once. You may pray for someone, see a person respond, sometimes see a miracle of salvation or healing. It is not often that you meet people again and see how they have continued in their walk with God. These two young ladies were now mature Christians and established members of their church. A testament to the steadfast love of God.

> *"'My food," said Jesus, "is to do the will of him who sent me and to finish his work. Don't you have a saying, 'It's still four months until harvest'? I tell you, open your eyes and look at the fields! They*

are ripe for harvest. Even now the one who reaps draws a wage and harvests a crop for eternal life, so that the sower and the reaper may be glad together. Thus the saying 'One sows and another reaps' is true. I sent you to reap what you have not worked for. Others have done the hard work, and you have reaped the benefits of their labour.'" (John 4:34–38 NIV)

A young lady in the meeting took photos of me and Dima. I still have those pictures today, as you can see.

the team would preach and share the gospel, people responded, signs and wonders followed and we would hear testimonies of what God had done. The night I ministered one lady came forward; she had back problems and all her pains went after prayer but for some reason she did not want to give her testimony. The next day she came to me and asked if I would pray for her husband's hands.

'Where is he?' I asked.

'Over there – he's in a fluorescent jacket, he is an usher,' she replied.

'Bring him over. What's wrong with his hands?' I asked.

The lady's husband came over to me.

'Look,' she said. His hands were obviously badly affected by arthritis; they were all bent and the joints gnarled. I was about to start to pray but as I looked down again his hands were straight. I looked up into a face which had the biggest of smiles. I had never seen anything quite like it before. I was used to seeing miracles *after* prayer but the way this happened took me totally by surprise. Many times a miracle can't be seen; it is only the recipient who can testify to it, such as when pain goes. This healing was instantaneous and visibly transformative and I just had to look again at God's miracle.

Tim and I travelled next to Belarus and back to Bulgaria where we ministered and taught in the mission schools together with Yauheni and Sofi. This time together before The Way Festival in England was to prove so beneficial. Yauheni was coming over with his family to help Tim with setting-up the tent. Sofi was coming over with her family for the women's meetings. Both would be taking part in the street evangelism.

> *'So if there is any encouragement in Christ, any comfort from love, any participation in the Spirit, any affection and sympathy, complete my joy by being of the same mind, having the same love, being in full accord and of one mind. Do nothing from rivalry or conceit, but in humility count others more significant than yourselves. Let each of you look not only to his own interests, but also to the interests of others. Have this mind among yourselves, which is yours in Christ Jesus.'*
> (Philippians 2:1–3,5 ESV)

Chapter 24

THE WAY FESTIVAL

When I think of a tent mission I immediately think 'freedom' and have the expectation of God touching lives.

The first tent mission I had ever seen or been involved with was in 1999 in Brentwood. In 2011 Yauheni had challenged me to bring a tent to England. I had shared the vision with church leaders in Brentwood and although some were initially sceptical about Yauheni leading the event because of his lack of English, when he came with his interpreter Vitali and preached an inspiring message from Psalm 34:8 ('Taste and see that the LORD is good') they were convinced.

Tim, in addition to owning the yellow-and-white mission tent we had used in 1999, also owned a 1500-seater blue-and-white tent which he thought would be more suitable for the new event. It had taken us two years but we had finally got agreement from the local churches that The Way Festival would be held at the end of July 2013.

With the date agreed the steering group, made up of leaders from four local churches, could really get into action; we had just a year to get everything, including the financial backing, in place. Tim was a great help with all the logistical requirements. He had done this sort of thing so many times and had it all well documented. In addition to the tent he also had a stage, sound, lighting, screens and some of the seating. He did not live locally but we had his expertise at the end of a phone.

Tim's documents highlighted the need for a large space with good access and plenty of parking. Ideally, we would have liked a neutral site but none of the available sites met Tim's requirements so it was agreed to pitch the tent in the grounds at the back of my home church which, although out of the town centre, did have plenty of space for parking and allowed us access to the church's generator.

It is always best to have the tent where the public can see it and this was the obvious disadvantage with our site. So now we had to find a means of attracting families, which we hoped to do by running activities when the tent meetings were not in session. Through the activities we aimed to publicise the outreach. We looked to book Tough Talk, a team of weight lifters, to share the gospel. We booked gospel bands to minister each night and our planning teams were organising a women's day and events specifically geared for children and youth.

God's ways are not always our ways. We had wanted to hold this event in 2012 but I can see now how God brought us all together and gave us a time to form bonds. I can see now the importance of the trip to Moscow where Tim met with Yauheni, Kevin and Leslie, and connected with delegates at the Tent 100 conference. God was making connections in the Kingdom. It was like a big spider's web linking people. Our travelling and ministering together as a team in Bulgaria, Macedonia and Russia was part of the preparation for The Way Festival. As it says in the Bible: 'Iron sharpens Iron' (Proverbs 27:17 NIV).

Between missions in Europe my time in England was focused on preparations for The Way. First we had to build a website. The programme was organised so now the advertising could be finalised and banners and posters put up around town and further afield. The website reached where physical notices couldn't. We were networking with churches and having opportunities to share on local radio and Christian TV. The leaflets were ready for the street evangelism teams.

Tim arrived with the big tent and under his direction a team of volunteers quickly erected it so the technicians could get to work on the sound and lighting systems.

Judy played a large part in organising the catering and providing hospitality for Tim and his wife Kim, Yauheni, Sofi and their families. I was pleased the spouses could finally meet together, the ones who stay behind and look after things when the evangelists go off on mission. Now we were one big family.

We took to the streets every day during the festival giving out flyers and inviting people to come. We had special times of encouragement, prayer and testimonies each day. A little illustration: I was sharing a leaflet and the gospel on the high street with a lady who was from Eastern Europe. It was getting to the point when I needed help because her English wasn't very good. She said she spoke Russian. I turned around and who was right behind me but Sofi who was able to lead her in the prayer of salvation in Russian. Little 'Godincidences' which were such an encouragement for everyone!

Keith and Jenny had come down from Blackpool to lead the worship so we had a lively start before the Tough Talk power lifters gave a demonstration of their skills and shared stories of their pasts and testimonies of how God came into their lives. The audience really got involved and the power lifters invited the young and fit to lift weights themselves. They made a real connection with some of the young men on that first night. And those young men returned with their friends later in the week.

The next evening Yauheni spoke, with Vitali interpreting. It was a powerful gospel message and people came forward for salvation and healing. Tim was the speaker the following evening and again we saw people responding as the gospel was preached. Some of the people who had been healed the previous night gave their testimonies, which encouraged others to come forward for prayer. We were blessed to have Keith and Jenny to lead the worship both before the preaching and during times of prayer.

On Wednesday afternoon Sofi, Kim and Kalbi Massey hosted a ladies' event, sharing their testimonies, addressing issues and answering questions from a woman's perspective.

As we had seen at other tent events the numbers of people coming gradually increased during the week as word got around. On Wednesday night Helen

Yousaf from Elim joined us to lead the worship and then it was my turn to speak. After I had shared my testimony and a gospel message many people came forward for prayer and many testified to being healed; body, soul and spirit as they were prayed for by the team. It is always difficult to remember every individual who received healing when there are so many but I do remember a lady called Elisa who came forward for healing. She had great pain in her neck and back and had, for some time, been receiving treatment from a chiropractor with no apparent improvement. God healed her in an instant. She was from a local church and was soon up on the stage giving her testimony of her healing, encouraging non-believers to come to the tent the next night and to go to church. I still see her occasionally; in fact her picture was on our second festival flyer in 2015.

On Friday we took the outreach into the centre of the town. George Osborn from Lumina Ministry set up a gazebo and tables and invited people to talk about the New Age and the occult. Many people came to the tent that evening to hear his testimony of how he got himself involved in drugs and the occult and how God had got him out and set him free. His story obviously resonated with many in the congregation and it was good to see people who were involved with these things coming forward and responding to the message. You can read George's testimony in his book *Out of Darkness*.

Saturday was our final day and we had a very full programme of events. We started early with a breakfast stall on site at which John Lawson told his story about how he found God whilst in prison. The Ark Bible Club provided a children's ministry with lots of music, games and Bible stories. Athletes in Action kept the youth busy with an engaging selection of sports intermingled with their Christian message. A lovely day was followed by an evening of celebration. Many folk who had come during the week gathered to worship but we had a large number of people coming to the tent for the first time. People were sharing their testimonies and giving thanks to God for touching their lives, for re-energising their Christian walk.

As the organising team reflected on the festival we concluded that it had been a success: many people had heard the truth of the gospel for the first time and become Christians; others re-dedicated their lives to God; others received healing. Many people had commented on the freedom that they had felt in the tent. It was truly an encouraging time.

Being part of the organising team made me realise how 'easy' it is for a travelling evangelist who turns up, does the job and leaves. Yes, travelling can be tiring but it is a very different sort of tiredness compared to organising an event when you work day after day to make sure all of the arrangements are in place and on time. It takes teamwork. The visitors are remembered, but it's the local team that get them onto the platform.

'I have planted, Apollos watered; but God gave the increase. So then neither is he that planteth any thing, neither he that watereth; but God that giveth the increase. Now he that planteth and he that watereth are one: and every man shall receive his own reward according to his own labour. For we are labourers together with God: ye are God's husbandry, ye are God's building.' (1 Corinthians 3:6–9)

What a blessing it is to serve. Opportunities come when we work together – a simple conversation when erecting or taking down the tent can be faith-building and sometimes life-changing. We don't always see what God is doing at the time but sometimes we do find out the impact our preaching has made. Some months after the festival I stopped at the roadside to buy some tomatoes. The man serving me said, 'I remember you; you were one of those preachers in that tent. I came every night to hear all of them. I'd never experienced anything like it. It has changed my life even though I was a churchgoer before!' More recently a mother reminded me that her teenaged daughter Stephanie had been saved in the tent the night Yauheni preached.

Chapter 25

MESSENGER – OTM

We are called to share the gospel, to share the love of Jesus. Opportunities come in all sorts of situations. It could be on a one-to-one basis or in front of an audience at a church event, at home or abroad. Since my return from Moscow I had been filled with such a boldness to declare the Good News and my whole being felt on fire on the inside. I had an expectation that when the gospel was preached signs and wonders would follow.

Many people will never enter a church and so we need to be messengers and take Jesus onto our streets. There are many people outside the church with broken lives, lonely people, people who need help. Many people in our churches have the gift of hospitality and the compassion to help others. Put these gifts and the power of God together and we have the ability to meet needs. Simply feed and talk to people, take the time to show them the love of Jesus and lives are changed. This is the philosophy behind the 'On the Move' (OTM) ministry.

On the Move has been running in Brentwood for a number of years. This is a regular outreach in the town and surrounding villages supported by Brentwood Churches Together. It is great to see the way people from various churches come together to share the love of Jesus in their community in a practical way. It is a barbecue ministry. For three days in early summer we occupy a little open space in the centre of town and set up grills and gazebos, set out tables and chairs and connect up the sound system. The catering team slice onions and bread rolls, grill burgers and sausages, and then for two hours in the middle of the day shoppers are offered a free burger or hot dog and a drink, and the opportunity to sit and chat or just listen to the Christian music. People often ask, 'Why is it free?' Our reply is, 'We want to share God's love in this community.'

In Brentwood there is a monument to a young man called William Hunter who, in 1555, was burnt at the stake for keeping his faith and refusing to recant his Protestant beliefs. Lately it has become even more infamous as a main location for the TV show *The Only Way is Essex* (TOWIE). What would William Hunter make of his home town now? In 2014, at the height of TV show's popularity, the town was a magnet for hen parties and stag nights, particularly at the weekends. That year, over the three days of On the Move we served a total of 1,070 burgers, 470 hot dogs and 96 veggie burgers, making in total 1,636 servings.

Three different music groups ministered during the outreach. On the first day Helen Yousaf was singing and leading some local musicians; the next day ECHO came along with their special brand of 'Soul and Motown' Christian adapted songs and on the Saturday the Trinity Singers and band performed a variety of gospel music.

Typically, people are attracted by the music. Some are drawn by the smell of the onions wafting down the high street. Some just respond to the friendly invitation to sit down and enjoy some free food and entertainment.

I want to share here some of my highlights of that particular On the Move.

What happened on the first day is the 'tallest story' I have ever told. A young man stopped to listen to the music as Helen was singing. He stood just behind me and I invited him to sit down and have a burger. He began by telling me he was an atheist.

'What made you stop?' I asked.

'It was the music.'

He agreed to have a burger and we sat and chatted some more. We talked about creation and life in general. He said he was a professional basketball player and coach from Portsmouth. He told me that he was missing his parents and sister and that he was concerned about them. I asked him how he had found his way to Brentwood. He said that he used a satnav. It was my cue to hand him my 'directions' tract. Then I suggested, 'We can pray for your family: that you will have a peace in your heart, and your parents and sister will have that same peace.'

'That would be nice,' he replied.

I prayed and then I gave him some space to read the tract and finish his burger. When I came back to him he seemed much more open and I shared my testimony using the 'tear and share' which ended up by him responding to the gospel. I will never forget Lawrence standing next to Helen and myself with a big smile on his face – all seven-foot-two-inches of him!

A number of the people who were prayed for that day had problems walking and after they were prayed for the pain went! At one point two of them were dancing because all the pain in their legs had disappeared. One of the dancers gave her life to Christ, as did his sister. Lesley was sitting on a bench as she told us she had a blood clot and had a lot of pain in her leg. When we prayed for her she reported that her leg became 'hot and the pain had gone'. We shared the gospel with her and she told me she was a lapsed Christian. She prayed, asking Jesus back into her life. It was a very fruitful first day.

Day Two and we were again blessed with glorious sunshine. ECHO played their special brand of music and once again people were stopping to listen and then began queuing to be served a burger or hot dog. The wonderful team of volunteers were inviting them to take a seat with their food and enjoy the band. We had people hosting tables, chatting with the guests, making them welcome. It always surprises folk when they not only get free food but that it's served caringly and lovingly.

Nina brought a young lad, George, to whom she had been talking about a youth ministry called Athletes in Action, over to where I was sitting. The youngster had told her he couldn't play sport because of his injuries. He had a brace on his arm. George and his mum sat down and Nina explained that

133

George loved sport but couldn't play because of his arm.

We were about to witness God's miraculous intervention into two lives.

George said that he was in continuous pain.

'George, can you remove your brace, and let me pray for Jesus to heal you?'

It was OK with George and it was OK with his mum.

I laid my hands on his arm and as I prayed I felt the heat flowing through my hands. I knew God had touched him.

George looked up at me, 'The pain has gone!' The big smile said more than his words.

I smiled back at George telling him that the Jesus who had healed him loved him so much. Then I shared the gospel using the 'tear and share' paper illustration. We talked for quite a while and as we prayed together George wanted to know how he could know about Jesus. I gave him a 'Why Jesus' booklet and a Bible.

After we prayed I asked him if everything was alright. George said, 'Yes, but my little finger hurts a bit.'

'Shall we pray again?' I asked.

We prayed again, and George said, 'It's gone.'

I said, 'Let's give God the thanks, shall we, George?'

Mum Kathy was blown away by what had happened to her son. Her eyes were full of tears which became visible on her cheeks. I stretched my hand forward and held her hand to reassure her that everything was OK.

Kathy looked up at me saying, 'My hand and arm had been tingling and painful until you touched me.' I hadn't prayed for Kathy at this stage, just simply touched her hand.

Kathy told me that she had diabetes. Her arm had been painful and she was suffering with 'paresthesia'– numbness and pins and needles. She asked me to pray for her. The pain in her arm had gone but I also prayed for the anxiety and depression. She told me she was angry with God. Kathy had witnessed God touch her physically; it was time to pray for her to receive peace in her heart and mind. I encouraged her to find a church. She told me she used to attend Christ Church, Warley. I knew Christ Church had a new vicar but I had never met him and didn't know who he was.

This was really a time of signs and wonders. I believe there are no coincidences, God always has a plan. My friend Gary Seithel, who leads the local On the Move, was talking to this big guy who was dressed in motorbike leathers and had a helmet in his hand. I interrupted to ask Gary if he knew who the new vicar at Christ Church was. Yes, his name was Rob and he just happened to be the biker! Rob had come to see how On the Move worked. This was God's perfect timing to introduce George and Kathy to the vicar!

Many other team members had the opportunity to pray with people, share testimonies, and give gospel tracts, the Father's Love Letter and invitations to Athletes in Action. All were buzzing with excitement at what God was doing.

Our son Kevin had pulled together a brilliant band and singers, mainly from our home church Trinity, for Saturday afternoon, our final day. The high street was very busy and the team was at full stretch serving and caring for people.

My friend Alan Cass called me over to meet a group of five lads from Norwich who were down for the weekend. Alan had been chatting with them eating burgers and hot dogs. Now he said: 'Peter, share your testimony with these lads, they're football fans.' I began telling the story of my days as a footballer, using the 'tear and share' origami. They were a friendly bunch with plenty of questions, especially when the word 'Hell' was made from the paper tear.

Then I rearranged the word Hell to spell LOVE. You could see the minds of two of the group working. Alan said, 'You have a choice, guys – don't they, Peter?'

'Yes, of course,' I said, as I held up another piece of paper. God's word says, 'For God so loved the world that he gave his one and only Son, that whoever believes in him shall not perish but have eternal life' (John 3:16 NIV).

I opened up the final piece of paper and unfolded it to reveal the cross. I told them that they now had a choice to make. Two immediately asked, 'What can I do?' So Alan and I shared and prayed with them as they individually all made a commitment to follow Christ.

Not long afterwards a group of girls on a hen party were invited to listen to the music and enjoy free burgers and hot dogs. They were a lively bunch from Leeds who were in town to let their hair down for the weekend. This time our conversation was centred on love. I gave each one of the seven girls a 'love tract' which started the girls chatting amongst themselves. Some just sat and read the tract through while others giggled and chatted. The Holy Spirit was certainly at work. I was prompted to say, 'Are you looking for perfect love, because it can only come from one place?'

They asked, 'From where?' It was my opening to tell them my story, using 'tear and share' to illustrate that perfect love can only come through God. Going through the same sequence of 'tears' and ending with the same scripture. 'Now girls, we all want to be loved, don't we?'

'Yes,' they all replied immediately.

'You can make a choice. It's simple: Jesus has already paid the price for you on the cross.' I handed the paper cross to the bride-to-be. It was amazing how the Holy Spirit used this trip to Brentwood for them to find out 'The only way is Jesus, not Essex' – Jesus said, 'I am the way and truth and the life' (John14: 6).

These were just some of the stories from three amazing days from one year's outreach. On the Move continues to provide wonderful opportunities to minister to the community. Working *together* is the key to this and other ministries. Using our different talents and letting the Holy Spirit work through us. I have made some great friends and seen God touch so many lives at these events. 'What a friend we have in Jesus!'

Reflection:

I just want to encourage you to use whatever gift God has given you to share that love. The smallest of kindly actions can have the most profound effect in a person's life.

me and Tim at the very end when the crowds had largely dispersed. We prayed for her physical healing and God gave me a word of knowledge that she wanted to respond to the gospel. She received Jesus and became number seventeen!

The Kids' Club each afternoon was a great success and the tent rang to the sound of 'Great Great Brill Brill' and other such lively songs learned from the Spearhead team. Faces were being transformed by the skill of the face painters and the bouncy castle was very popular. The children were so receptive and really enjoyed the interaction with Joe Crow as he taught them memory verses such as John 3:16 through my interpreter Venny.

Despite the heat and humidity, the evening meetings were well attended. We continued to see people responding to the gospel message as Sofi, Tim and I preached. At each event some of the team members shared how knowing God had impacted their lives. On Sunday morning the team divided into four smaller groups and dispersed around the region to minister in various churches; the presence and power of God was manifested and many lives were touched and people were healed.

I went off with Colin, Stanislav and Venny. I preached from Isaiah 53 – Christ's willingness to face undeserved suffering on our behalf that brought us salvation and healing – before sharing my personal testimony. Over half of the church responded to receive Jesus and it was wonderful to see many get healed and a blessing to hear their testimonies.

The final evening culminated with a time of anointing and prayer for baptism in the Holy Spirit. As the last person walked through the prayer tunnel I looked around the tent to see many children and adults sitting or standing weeping in the Spirit, such was the presence of God in the tent. People quite simply didn't want the time to end.

We struck the tent by the light of our car headlights, finally getting everything stowed in the early hours of Monday morning and then it was time to say our goodbyes. After only a few hours' sleep the English team had to set off for Sofia to catch the plane back to the UK ready for work at 7 a.m. on Tuesday morning.

What was so evident was the unity of all the folk from England, Bulgaria, and the local Romany ministries. People working together and supporting each other with just the one aim of seeing Jesus transform lives.

A few months later I was back in Bulgaria, this time in Blagoevgrad, a city in the south-west of the country. On the mountainside above the urban sprawl is a cross which can be seen from miles around. At night time it is illuminated so it is visible 24-hours a day. Once you have seen it, you can never forget it. It is a reminder that Jesus died for us all and He is with us all day, every day.

This was my second visit to the city: in autumn the previous year we had held a 'Time to GO' mission school to equip local Christians with evangelism and mission skills. Now, in May 2015, we were back to hold a tent mission in the centre of town. Tim had again organised a team from Spearhead Ministries to support the Bulgarian Tent 100 team who were running the mission.

We began by leading teams out on the street to evangelise locally and helping with the children's ministry each day. Tim, Sofi and I preached on alternate evenings, and local musicians would lead the worship. We saw people respond to the gospel messages and signs and wonders followed as people received healing and salvation.

On my last day with the mission we went to the top of the mountain which was a breathtaking experience. From mountaintop to valley though, as we arrived at the tent to be told that a complaint had been made to the mayor's office, as a result of which we weren't allowed to hold a religious meeting; so no microphones and no musicians. As a local pastor explained the situation to the people who had gathered I began to pray and I was inspired to share a message from John 8:12 where Jesus said, 'I am the light of the world.' I began to talk without a microphone: 'If I was allowed to speak this is what I would share . . .' So people got to hear the message in and amongst my farewell words.

The humid weather gave way to a tremendous rainstorm which was followed by brilliant sunshine. When we looked outside the tent, we saw a double rainbow in the sky! I had really felt God's presence as I was sharing and saying goodbye. I was confident God would also cause the ruling to be overturned, which he did a few days later after Sofi, Tim and local ministers got their audience with the mayor's office. Glory to God. The team was back ministering again.

Back in England

In the summer of 2015 we were back in Brentwood with the second Way Festival. For months the steering group had been planning and connecting with the local churches to partner with this mission. We shared with them how we had seen evidence of God's word and work breaking out all over Europe following tent ministry. Our testimony was one of faith. Again, we were stepping out in faith in response to the great commission to 'Go ye into all the world and preach the gospel . . . Working with them, and confirming the word with signs following' (Mark 16:15, 20). We had a good number of churches pledging to support the event, with Tim once again supplying the tent.

We displayed banners at partnering churches, put up posters in pet shops and fish-and-chip shops around town. We were focused on getting the message out and used many forms of media. This included appearing on SKY Ben TV with Anna Trehern, who helped me with marketing, and Tim and I speaking on Phoenix FM Radio to promote the event. The Way Festival had its own Facebook page and website (www.thewayfestival.com); they're still live so you can pick up on events. We published profiles and accounts of those speaking. Gary Seithel, of the steering group, would publish short reports on the sense of God's presence. Wonderful times of worship; as many churches were represented, local pastors would welcome people and the speakers each evening.

We took to the streets with leaflets designed to look like a tent and we had many interesting encounters when giving invitations to people. One notable instance was a lady who came from quite a distance away in Kent. She said she was interested in coming but truthfully, we didn't expect to see her. Our scepticism was ill-founded: she came with her four teenage children all of whom eventually made a decision to receive Jesus. In fact they came every night and brought other members of the family.

We invited spirit-filled bands representing various ministries to lead the worship each evening. We had special events for the youth, ladies and men. For the men's event we had invited Jimmy Tibbs to share his boxing ring testimony, during which two older ladies were saved and healed, proving God's ways are not always our ways!

Gary Seithel wrote this short report to some local ministries:

The theme seemed to be 'The God of the Unexpected!' Mary and her friend wanted to hear Jimmy Tibbs – a top boxing trainer from the East End of London – talk about his life and faith. Mary had known the family years ago and her neighbours invited them. This was Saturday at a men's breakfast! We hoped some men would respond but both of these older ladies prayed to receive Christ at the end! They then asked about God healing today. Mary had fallen and badly hurt her back. Peter and I prayed for her . . . she tested it and it was fine! Her friend said, 'Pray for ME! I have breathing problems.' As we prayed for her breathing, it became easier and both of them continue to grow in grace.

Another unexpected outcome was a flyer Peter gave to a woman from Kent . . . she said 'I'll be coming to that!' Peter admits his thoughts were more, 'I'll never see her there.' The surprise was when she did come and bring her four children. Then her brother came as well almost every night! It turns out Margaret had recently lost her husband and needed the prayers and encouragement. Her son, Tommy, rededicated his life to Christ. The three younger ones all gave their lives to Jesus for the first time! Her brother Larry felt the 'time is now' to get his life recommitted to Christ.

Every night some came to Christ for the first time, others rededicated their lives, and others came forward for prayer where the Father did amazing things! Bernadette hasn't been able to kneel for decades . . . she now has no pain or stiffness in her knees! Alan had back pain and it has been completely fine since receiving prayer at the festival. We heard testimonies of people whose acid reflux was completely better; of depression that has lifted; of a deeper sense of confidence in God. Nicki gave testimony of her knees and arm being healed and instead of discouragement, depression and anxiety, found a new peace in her heart from Christ. Please pray for those who have come to Christ and seen answers to prayer to continue to grow in their faith and walk of discipleship.

We continued to hear testimonies and stories of how God touched lives; these were still filtering through weeks later.

Tim was ministering one night to a whole row of young men from a Teen Challenge (London) centre; a number of them responded and two received healing. My friend John was ushering that night. A year later John visited a Teen Challenge centre in Nottingham and a young man there recognised him. The man told John that the time in the tent was the turning point for him, allowing him to take the first steps in breaking free from his past. Two years ago I was in the middle of Brentwood and a lady came up to me and said, 'You are from that big tent. I was prayed for and I had cancer. The doctor has now told me I have no sign of cancer.' She is now in a church with her sister and family and delights in telling her testimony of how God healed her.

God's grace never ceases to amaze me. The Way Festival was a lot of hard work but it brought a tremendous unity and blessing to those who got involved. Fellow Christians often ask us how many people are saved and healed. My response is always the same: every night hundreds of people heard the truth of the gospel and my Bible says that when the gospel is shared, signs and wonders follow (Mark 16:20).

'For it is by grace you have been saved, through faith; and that not of yourself; it is a gift of God.' (Ephesians 2:8)

The Way, the Truth, and the Life

'Truly, truly, I say to you, whoever believes in me will also do the works that I do; and greater works than these will he do, because I am going to the Father. Whatever you ask in my name, this I will do, that the Father may be glorified in the Son. If you ask me anything in my name, I will do it.' (John 14:12–14 ESV)

Chapter 27

ON TRACK, BURNING PASSION

My brother-in-law Sunny and his wife Connie were on holiday with us in the UK for New Year in 2014. I asked the question that was burning in my heart:

'What's the latest from the jungle? What's been happening?'

'Forty-two of the tribe have been baptised,' Sunny said.

'I have a burning passion to return.'

'Well get in contact with Bobby and ask him if you can accompany him on a trip.'

It was a long way to travel but Judy and Connie really encouraged me to get in contact with Bobby and GO!

I phoned Bobby and his immediate response was, 'Yes, please come!' I could sense there was an underlying excitement, not just enthusiasm in his response. Then he continued: 'Peter, would you consider coming with me to Siem Reap in Cambodia? I have been there several times. I believe we could see a similar breakthrough as the local pastor goes out into the villages. He has around sixteen villages and goes with a team. It's called "The Church of God, Siem Reap".'

I said I would pray about it and let him know what I thought God wanted me to do. I had always wanted to return again to the Orang Asli people in the Malaysian jungle. I had already visited them three times and I had continued to pray for them (and of course I still do). I believe it was Leb's miracle on my first trip that began my outreach ministry called Zeal. After praying I believed that this really was God's timing for me to go, and confirmation came when I received an invitation from the Cambodian pastor, Pastor Kundate, to hold a mission school for his team. He wanted me to teach on 'The Great Commission'.

Putting Cambodia into the itinerary would obviously mean a longer trip as we would be spending a week with Pastor Kundate. We began to make plans: the only dates which worked for all of us came straight after the week I was due to be in Bulgaria on a mission. This meant I would only get to see Judy for four days before I would be off again for just over three weeks. This was not ideal but Judy had been praying too and she encouraged me to go.

I had a longstanding invitation to visit Dr Philip Lyn of Skyline Church in Kota Kinabalu (KK) the next time I was in Malaysia, so I called him to see if he would be in Sabah during the time of my proposed trip. He invited me to be his house guest if I could fit KK into my schedule. I left London on a Friday evening and arrived in Kuala Lumpur on the Saturday afternoon. The next morning I had to be up at 4 a.m. to catch an early flight to KK so that I would be in time to hear Philip preach. His message was 'Alive Again' and was just the 'food' I needed at the start of the mission trip. One simple sentence in particular resonated with me: *'We often make a decision, but a decision is different from a commitment.'* It was truly a blessed time of fellowship for me in preparation for the journeys in Cambodia and Malaysia that lay ahead.

Amazing Sovereign God

Back again in Kuala Lumpur and I was staying with Bobby and Fiona who had invited me to use their home as my base. Bobby had booked our flight to Siem Reap and organised the hotel rooms. We were collected from the airport by Pastor Kundate who took us to the hotel in his Jeep – but only to drop off our bags. Back in the Jeep and we were off to his church to meet his team and within ten minutes we were heading out into the villages to see the outreach ministries in progress.

Cambodia is a Buddhist country and Pastor Kundate and his wife have governmental permission to go out into the rural areas to teach English.

On the first evening we stopped at a total of eight villages and, towards the end, we were driving in pitch-black darkness, bouncing around on very uneven roads. As we arrived back in the city I looked across at Pastor Kundate and it was obvious that he was in a lot of pain. I asked him if he was OK and he admitted that his back

and legs were actually in agony as he drove. He had been seriously injured several years previously but had learned to live with the pain. Obviously bouncing around in a Jeep on potholed roads did nothing to help matters. Bobby and I, having left Kuala Lumpur on an early-morning flight, were hungry and very tired. We stopped for something to eat and then Pastor Kundate dropped us at our hotel, exhausted and ready to sleep.

The next morning we were collected at 8.30 a.m. and taken to Pastor Kundate's church, where I was to teach on 'The Great Commission'. The event was to run for a week with seminar sessions during the daytime and visiting villages during the evenings to minister to children and their parents. I had come well stocked with resources including the Ark Bible Club children's DVD, Christianity Explored material, books, tracts, teaching aids and a projector.

Pastor Kundate welcomed us and then Bobby introduced me to the twenty-four students. As I was about to begin I noticed Pastor Kundate was in great pain once more as he moved to sit with us around the long table.

'Pastor Kundate, are you OK?'

'No,' he replied.

God was prompting me to pray for him.

'Can I pray for you, Pastor?' I laid my hands on the base of his spine and immediately he said that his back was becoming hot. I asked him to move around to test whether he still had pain.

Bobby said, 'Try to touch your toes,' which Pastor Kundate did and replied with a somewhat surprised look on his face, 'It's a bit better.' We asked him

to continue moving around to try to find the pain. Then I felt a prompting again: 'Jump as high as you can, raising your knees.' Wow! he jumped as high as the seat he had been sitting on. Then he touched his toes again.

First a big smile, then he said, 'My pain has gone, I have no pain. God has miraculously healed me!'

What a great way to start to the day, the seminar, the week!

The group settled down as we started the first session on 'The Great Commission' with me explaining that it is one of the most significant passages in Scripture, that it is the last recorded personal instruction given by Jesus to His disciples and it is a special calling to all His followers to take specific action while on this earth (Matthew 28:16–20).

Adventure

The pastor was arranging to hold a crusade in the largest of the villages that he visited and in the afternoon he wanted to take us there to show us the preparations. The journey itself was a real adventure. We travelled in two Jeeps on dirt roads strewn with large potholes with rice paddy fields on either side. Suddenly we crashed down into a pothole and, as the Jeep struggled out again, it was obvious that the steering had been badly damaged. We were miles from anywhere so it was an off-road repair. The wheel was changed, the steering joint repaired and we were on our way again to the sound of crickets and other creatures.

The road came to an end and the only way forward was through the river ahead. We crawled down the bank and into the river, the nose of the Jeep slowly disappearing under the water as we inched our way down the incline. Then the slope levelled off and we could see the end of the bonnet again but now the water rushed in through the open doors, and suddenly my feet were extremely wet. We finally arrived at the opposite bank and, thank God, the Jeep kept going steadily to the top of the incline; as it did so the water sloshed into the back of the vehicle but everyone there had seen my discomfort and lifted their feet up so they didn't get wet. It was a really exciting experience although I do remember hoping there were no snakes or alligators in the river. As we reached the top we all burst out laughing, partly in relief and partly at my wet feet!

We stopped for a while to let the water run out of the vehicle before setting off again along the unmade road beside the riverbank. We heard the wildlife around us as we bumped along our way, and gradually the road turned away from the river and the paddy fields and led us through some small settlements where the dogs came out to bark at us.

At first the road was just tree-lined but then the depth of the trees increased and the road began to twist and turn even more. It seemed that there were a lot more settlements after we had entered the wooded area. The villages were getting larger; some of them had motorbikes parked outside the houses. Eventually we came to our destination, the village where we would be holding the crusade. There were many more houses in this village, as well as large barns where the rice was stored after it had been harvested.

We were met by a large group of young people, some of whom had been with us at the ministry seminars back in Siem Reap. They were so excited at our arrival and they had prepared a welcome for us. There were around fifty young children to whom they had been teaching English and gospel action songs. The place was absolutely buzzing with excitement. The ministry students had put together a great programme; we used an amplifier so that the sound would travel and the local people would become aware that something exciting would be happening in the next few days. Advertising rural Cambodian style! After a great evening it was time to return to the city once again.

We returned to the village a few days later for the start of the crusade. It was a two-hour drive from Siem Reap and, on the way, I asked Pastor Kundate to stop at a roadside market as I needed a torch for my illustration 'Jesus is the Light the world'. Then we were back on those unmade roads and through that river again, although this time I was prepared for the water coming through the doors and lifted my feet out of the way. The water soon drained away through drain holes in the floor as we continued on our bumpy way along the track to the village.

We received a wonderful welcome and I believe the number of people who had gathered surprised Pastor Kundate. At the front the children, from smallest to tallest, sat on a big mat. The parents were behind the children and around the perimeter people were looking out from buildings. People just kept turning up, even after the children started to sing their actions songs. Those children just melted my heart!

Pastor Kundate introduced Bobby from Malaysia and then he introduced me as coming from England, travelling on a plane for fifteen hours to Malaysia and almost three hours to Cambodia. I began to share with them how Bobby

and I had met, how he had taken me into the jungle and how God had healed a little girl called Leb. I told them how the tribe's men were frightened because of my white skin and that made everyone laugh. Then Joe Crow came out to share the Lord's Prayer with the children and parents and, as usual, he grabbed everyone's attention, young and old.

I briefly related how I became a Christian and about my experience of God's love for me. Then I began to share the gospel and the cross with them. I spoke about our need to turn from sin and the power of darkness. I used the contrast of light and dark to illustrate Jesus being the Light of the world: 'God is light, and in Him is no darkness at all' (1 John 1:5) – I shone the torch around to demonstrate that it could bring light into darkness. I shared that Jesus said, 'I am the way, the truth, and the life' (John 14:6).

It was wonderful to see so many hands raised as they prayed to receive Jesus as their Saviour. God had done something special as they responded to His Word. People were being miraculously healed. At first just a few came forward, but as they shared their testimonies of God's healing touch, others came forward to be prayed for and have hands laid on them. Arms, hands, necks, backs, deaf ears, legs, breathing problems, stomach pains, headaches and blurred vision – all healed. There was a continuous stream of people. I can only think that word of what was happening had gone around the villages. It was getting late and still people were arriving. It was very hot and I was drenched in sweat as people surrounded us, some wanting to testify to what God had done and others wanting prayer. It was physically impossible to pray for everyone individually so I raised my hand and prayed for the group as a whole.

Bobby had brought food and medication for the people so we could show love to them in a practical way before we left. Then it was time to set off back to the city, including the river crossing in the pitch dark; as you can imagine this caused great excitement once more. It had been an amazing night and as we bumped our way back we were singing and rejoicing, praising God for the wonderful things He had done. It was a night I will never forget, seeing how our Sovereign God performed countless miracles as people were saved and healed.

The day after we got back to Siem Reap Bobby organised a celebration meal with the whole team. He was leaving the next day for Malaysia; I was staying on for a few more days' training with the students before following him back to Kuala Lumpur.

I had seen how the friendly Cambodian people greeted one another with a bow, their two hands together as if they were going to pray, and God laid it on my heart to print some hand tracts with the Lord's Prayer. They had been well received out in the villages but there people understood a little English. I asked Pastor Kundate to take me to printers in Siem Reap to see if they could produce the tracts in Cambodian. We eventually found a printer who could use my files. Pastor Kundate's wife translated the text

into the Khmer language and the presses were ready to roll. I was excited that I was able to produce 5,000 tracts that would be used to sow the gospel and the Lord's Prayer in the city as well as the villages.

Pastor Kundate treated me to a trip to the Angkor Wat, the world's largest religious monument, and a boat trip to show me some of the culture of the river boat people whose whole livelihood comes from fishing. My last meal in Cambodia was a barbecue served in a restaurant for just ten dollars. I had to try the local produce: meats, fish and crocodile. My mind went back to the river crossing in the Jeep. The meat tasted OK, but a bit gritty!

It had been an amazing time working with everyone in the mission school and sharing practically in the villages. I would have loved to go back to the village but my schedule was to return to Kuala Lumpur on Thursday to do my laundry and repack my bags ready for the next part of my trip.

Spirit of the Lord

Early Saturday morning I was heading for Kuala Lumpur railway station to start the 250km journey to Ipoh. My host, Revd Frank Lin, was there waving in greeting as I walked through the barrier at Ipoh station. The last time I had seen Frank was in Brentwood when he had come for a meal at my house. Straight away Frank took me to see the Ipoh Tree, which was immediately in front of the station, and he took some pictures to record my visit. Our next stop was St John's Church, the oldest Anglican church in Ipoh and now a listed building, where he had arranged for the vicar to show me around.

Then it was on to St Peter's Church where Frank is the vicar. He gave me details of the very full programme he had planned for me but I also needed to catch up with Judy's cousins and her Auntie Choo. With all the plans finalised we set off.

Frank's programme also included treating me to a trip around the city to sample some of the famous Ipoh cuisine, by the end of which I was absolutely stuffed by Frank's generosity and hospitality.

Back at the vicarage there was time for a shower and quick nap before Judy's cousins and auntie came to collect me for the evening. I enjoyed a really good time talking with Judy's cousins but I was shocked at Auntie Choo's lack of mobility as I had not seen her for a number of years. I asked if I could pray for her and the Holy Spirit touched her, relieving her pain. We had a wonderful time of prayer together before Dennis took me back to the vicarage. It was such a brilliant end to my first day in Ipoh.

I had to be up at 6.00 a.m. the next morning to get my bags packed because our schedule was so full I wouldn't have time to return to the vicarage before catching the train that evening. Frank took me for a dim sum breakfast before church, another epicurean delight although I left the chickens' feet for Frank to enjoy by himself!

St Peter's holds services in several different languages and I was due to speak at the English service at 9.00 a.m. Following a time of worship, Revd Frank introduced me to the congregation using downloads from the Zeal Outreach website. Then the lights went out and the computer stopped working due to a power failure. Immediately the elders began to pray. It was dark in the room and quickly started getting hot, so people began to open the curtains and windows. Revd Frank called out to the elders, 'Ask everyone to link hands and pray for the electricity to be restored'. Everyone began to pray aloud together and within a few minutes the electricity was back on and I was invited to the platform.

I had seen at the vicarage a leaflet about a discipleship course that Frank was planning to hold, so I had worked on a message to link with this. I felt God had given me a clear message for the church that day, which was in two parts.

I began with the question 'What is a Missionary?' and I shared what I feel is the foundational scripture:

'Jesus said to them again, ". . . As the Father has sent Me, I also send you"' (John 20:21 NKJV)

I started by reading from something I had written previously when asked to explain what I felt my call was as a missionary:

> A missionary is someone sent by Jesus Christ just as God sent Him. The great controlling factor is not the needs of people, but the command of Jesus. The source of our inspiration in our service for God is He is behind us, not ahead of us. The tendency today is to put the inspiration out in front – to sweep everything together in front of us and make it conform to our definition of success.

> But in the New Testament the inspiration is put behind us, and is the Lord Jesus Himself. The goal is to be true to Him – to carry out His plans. Personal attachment to the Lord Jesus and to His perspective is the one thing that must not be overlooked.

> In missionary work, the great danger is that God's call will be replaced by the needs of the people, to the point that human sympathy for those needs will absolutely overwhelm the

become deaf in one ear and had gone to the doctor who said she had an inner-ear infection. She had gone back to the doctor because the medication had not worked but nothing could be done to restore her hearing. She had come forward for prayer: 'You put your hands on my ears and the power of the Holy Spirit came on me. I fell.' She had felt her ear pop and when she stood up she could hear again.

I was still trying to leave but I was stopped again, this time by a man saying his knee was healed. I promised a tract to all those who had responded for salvation and I gave a bundle to the deacons to share with the folk. It was now past 11 a.m., the time that Frank and I were supposed to be at another church. I couldn't lay hands on everyone individually so I prayed over the rest of the group who had come forward. As I walked past them to the door I noticed some were slain in the Spirit and the church elders and deacons went to pray with them. This was the second time on the trip that I prayed for a group of people en masse but it was the first time in my ministry that I had witnessed the Holy Spirit moving in such a way. It was wonderful to be part of God's amazing grace at St Peter's that morning as God's anointing of the Holy Spirit flowed in His church.

Frank and I had to make our way quickly by car to 'Gereja Hallelujah', a Chinese church he looks after. By the time we arrived, the praise and worship phase of the service had already finished and the lady vicar was speaking. Frank led the Holy Communion service in English and Chinese for the twenty to thirty people who came forward to break bread.

After Communion, Frank introduced me as the speaker from England. It was nice to be working directly with Frank as he interpreted for me. I had been praying about what I should share and felt led to Isaiah 61: 'The Spirit of the Sovereign LORD is on me, because the LORD has anointed me to proclaim good news to the poor . . . bind up the broken-hearted . . . proclaim freedom for the captives . . .'(NIV). This seemed especially fitting after the tremendous anointing we had seen at St Peter's church. Frank read Isaiah 61 in Chinese.

It was an international audience. I had come from afar to bring the Word of God – I began by letting Joe Crow out of the bag again. He brought immediate laughter as he squawked and darted back into the bag coming out with a 'Praying Hands' tract in his beak. Frank, assisted by Joe, led everyone in the Lord's Prayer in Chinese.

I shared with the church what I had been doing since leaving England. I told them how I had become a Christian myself, and the fact that I was married to a Malaysian Chinese woman who was born near Ipoh was obviously a mark in my favour.

I realised my message needed to be short and to the point. I began by asking them about what it was to sin and if they knew if they would be going to heaven. I told them that Jesus only came for sinners like us or, as Luke puts it, '[He] came to seek and to save the lost' (Luke 19:10 NIV).

This led straight into leading questions like, 'Have you ever told a lie?' If they had, I said they should raise their hands, and I raised my own hand to demonstrate. Then: 'Have you ever taken something that doesn't belong to you?' again hands were raised including mine. I produced a piece of white paper and shared my 'tear and share' illustration with them. I shared John 3:16 as the paper revealed the word LOVE and told them that God sent Jesus because He loved them.

I asked them to indicate by raising their hand if they wanted to make a decision to come into relationship with their heavenly Father. Almost half of them responded. As Frank lead them in the prayer of repentance I unfolded the last piece of paper to reveal a cross. You could hear 'Oooo' or something similar in Chinese.

My body was feeling on fire as I prayed for people and God intervened in lives, saving and healing just as He had earlier at St Peter's. After the service we stayed on to fellowship, sharing home-cooked food and enjoying the lovely family atmosphere of the congregation.

I had so much to reflect on, seeing how the Holy Spirit had moved in each church service. People ask the question: 'Are signs and wonders "miracles" for today?' Most emphatically 'Yes!' God had given me such a boldness to share His Word, the Holy Spirit had led the way with signs and wonders, I had just been obedient in stretching forth my hand as a point of contact to allow healing in the name of Jesus. All I can say is that God did it. The Holy Spirit led everything! What a brilliant weekend. What a privilege to witness the awesome power of the Holy Spirit. I saw new things, or rather I didn't actually see all that God had done as people had fallen, 'slain in the spirit', as I walked by. I heard later via social media and email.

Return to the Jungle

Faithful Bobby met me at the station and took me to his home for a much-needed shower, a snack and sleep.

Pastor Kundate had arrived from Cambodia and now we loaded up Bobby's four-wheel drive with our clothes, bedrolls, large containers of drinking water, petrol for generators and 'supplies'. We had been to a supermarket the day before to buy perishable items for the tribe and I wanted to use some of the money supporters of my ministry had given me to bless the Orang Asli. We needed to buy for fifteen families, which is a lot of people when you consider that Ida, Leb's mum, has eight children. We set off on the 200km drive from Kuala Lumpur to Kuala Lipis where we stopped again to buy dry goods: staples such as rice, sugar and canned meat. I decided to buy some 'treats' to take to the villagers: banana, coconut and chocolate sponge logs. Bobby asked, 'What made you buy that particular cake?'

'The description on the wrapper sounded good.'

Bobby said, 'That's the one I normally buy, they love it!' They certainly did!

After Kuala Lipis we left the paved highway and followed dirt roads through a plantation. We were watching carefully to spot the dabs of coloured paint on the trees to make sure we were on the right track. The road was very bumpy with lots of twists and turns and it was a relief when we eventually came to the clearing, but what a difference now that we could drive all the way in to the village. The village had changed considerably since my first visit back in 2008, six years before. Above the huts were storage tanks to provide a supply of clean water, as well as brick-built toilet and shower blocks. Much of these improvements to the tribe's welfare is due to Bobby who has also been instrumental in getting them access to ID cards so that they can receive benefits and healthcare.

We arrived to such a welcome; people gathered round the car with wonderful smiles on their faces. Bobby had told them a week or so before that the 'white man' was coming! I recognised many of the adults who had received Jesus on my last visit. Ida was there in the front with her usual beaming smile, clutching her latest child. Every time I moved, there was Ida with that wonderful smile in front of me. I was bursting to see Leb but she was in the big community hut with the rest of the children having Sunday school. I had been waiting for years to see her again; I could wait a little longer.

A good number of the tribe had gathered under the trees; some were sitting on chairs, others on the verandas of surrounding huts. Bobby introduced Pastor Kundate who had been there once before, and asked him to pray for the tribe and then for their pastor, Pastor Suri, and his assistant.

I was asked to speak on what it means to be baptised and I shared a passage from the Gospel of Matthew:

'Then Jesus came to them and said, "All authority in heaven and on earth has been given to me. Therefore go and make disciples of all nations, baptising them in the name of the Father and of the Son and of the Holy Spirit, and teaching them to obey everything I have commanded you. And surely I am with you always, to the very end of the age."'
(Matthew 28:18–20 NIV)

I was honoured to be asked to assist Pastor Suri to baptise the eight people who made the decision to show their commitment to being part of the family of God. Pastor Suri had organised the filling of a small brick-built tank made specifically for this purpose. I was grateful that Bobby had asked him to fill the tank earlier in the day as the water came straight from the river and by now the sun had taken the chill off it. I was delighted to be back amongst the Oran Asli, especially at such a special time.

After the baptism Bobby wanted me to minister to the people again and pray for those who needed healing. As they came forward God touched many of them instantly. Many of the women had back problems, not really surprising as sometimes they were carrying two children, often with one feeding. God again gave me a word of knowledge – that someone had leg problems. Immediately this was translated, a group of the villagers came up to me. Pastor Suri explained to Bobby that I needed to go to a hut and pray for a man who had been mauled by a bear. We walked down to his hut and I stooped under the door lintel to see a man lying on a mat. I couldn't be sure but he looked like one of the men who had received Jesus in 2010.

He had been mauled on the lower shin and ankle. You could see the bone of the leg and claw marks on his foot. Amazingly he had managed to get away but it was a really deep, ugly wound. He had already had two miracles: he had escaped from the bear and there was no gangrene in the wound. Now I prayed for God's miracle healing touch so he could walk again. It had been a terrifying experience for the man and I felt to hug him and tell him how much God loved him. Bobby interpreted for me as I laid hands on him and prayed that God would heal and restore him. I was thinking that if God didn't touch him he would lose his leg or die. Before we left the village I prayed with him again and now he lifted his head and smiled! God is so awesome – two days later the man was up and walking about.

After the service came the celebration meal and whilst the preparations were being made it was my time to go and join the children and see Leb. The children were having great fun singing away and I was treated to lively Christian action songs – what a transformation in six years. Then it was time for Joe Crow to appear to share the Lord's Prayer. The children had met him before and soon they were joining in with him. I wanted to take a picture of Leb but she was very shy and reserved, although I knew she remembered who I was and she was happy to accept the Zeal t-shirt I had brought for her.

The food was now cooked and ready to serve. It smelled really good: large pots of rice, chicken in sauce, green vegetables, dried fish and wild boar that they caught in the jungle especially for our visit. The people had great appetites and there was plenty to go around. The wild boar was especially tasty although I did give the dried fish a miss. Next was the cake I'd bought in town: Bobby began to cut it in thick slices and it was delicious. He needed to remind them to take only one slice until everyone had had a piece!

It was almost time to be on our way. It was very hot and I was standing under the trees as Bobby distributed the medical supplies that he had brought with him: vitamins, worming tablets, dressings and various creams. People were coming to stand by me and smile; when you cannot speak the language, a hug says a lot. It was time to pray with the tribe and then be on our way. I felt so privileged and blessed to see what God was doing with His people in the jungle through some faithful disciples.

We set off back through the jungle following Pastor Suri and his team in the mini bus to their village about an hour's drive away. The temperature in Bobby's vehicle was 37oC and that was in the shade of the trees. Pastor Suri's village was not deep in the jungle but, nevertheless, it was well off any paved road and surrounded by woodland. There was a mixture of traditional wooden buildings and new brick buildings including toilet and shower blocks. I was surprised to see a reasonable-sized church building. The good news was that we were going to sleep on a wooden floor and not in a hut with a dirt floor!

I was going to speak to another group of villagers that night but first, yes, more food. Pastor Suri prepared a meal for everyone. I was really surprised to see a group of women and children whom I recognised walk out from the jungle. They had made their way from the village we had been at previously to come to the services. They would stay overnight at the other end of the church.

The service began with praise and worship and gradually more and more people arrived, including a group from a Chinese church that supported Pastor Suri. I shared a similar message to the one in Cambodia about Jesus being the Light of the world, once again illustrating it with a torch to show the difference between living in darkness and living in the light. It was good to see so many respond to the gospel. I then began to pray for the sick and many of them were healed, including the lead guitarist and the pastor's mother. I later learned from Pastor Suri that some of those who responded had previously turned away from the church and he was delighted that they were restored to God.

It was an interesting night and, I have to say, not the best sleep I have ever had. We slept on the floor of the church. The Orang Asli children woke a few times during the night and let everyone know about it and then at 4 a.m. the roosters started their morning crowing competition which reverberated from one end of the village to the other. Bobby, Kundate and I were awake, there was no point in trying to sleep anymore, so it was time to get up and shower. I spent some time reading my devotional and praying for the Holy Spirit to move on the meeting that day. I knew that I would mainly be speaking to people who had already given their lives to Christ and I felt to share the basic Christian message of Love being the root to the Christian faith. Then my mind drifted towards food and I had a real desire for scrambled eggs on toast and a strong black coffee. We had been invited to the pastor's house for breakfast and guess what he was making for everyone: scrambled eggs, cooked tinned ham, bread and seriously black coffee. We took the food up to the church to serve the people who had travelled so far to be with us.

Sunday morning's service began with Assistant Pastor Alfred leading the singing and Pastor Suri on the drums. Bobby introduced Pastor Kundate and then I shared the message I had prepared. I felt God was telling me to leave the platform and tell everyone to join me and stand by the big tree painted on the wall at the back of church. I asked the people what they could see when they looked at the tree and what they couldn't see. The first part they answered easily: they could see the trunk, the branches and the leaves. The second question was a little more difficult. I explained that you can't see the root but without it the tree cannot survive, without it there is no life. I went on to explain that we needed to be deeply rooted in love in Jesus Christ (Ephesians 3:17–19).

I asked two people to give testimonies of how God in His love had healed them the previous night and then the Holy Spirit began to lead me with words of knowledge. People, including Pastor Suri, were being slain in the Spirit and others were being healed. A young girl stood up and told us that she was tormented in mind; her tears were transformed to smiles as the Holy Spirit touched her and set her free.

I had given to Pastor Suri some resources for his ministry and he assured me they would be put to good use in his churches and in the outreach in the Orang Asli villages. It was so hard to say farewell: it was a very emotional time for me as people gathered around the car. As we pulled away Leb gave me a shy smile, so unlike her mother Ida's beaming face, but a smile nonetheless. I was absolutely exhausted as we drove back to Kuala Lumpur where Fiona was eagerly waiting to hear our news of what God had been doing amongst the Orang Asli. I had to pack for home so I needed to do some last-minute shopping for lobster crackers, banana cake and green cake for the grandchildren, before the taxi came to take me to the airport.

My flight home was scheduled to depart at 3 a.m. and fortunately I was able to sleep for most of the seven-hour flight to Abu Dhabi as I was so tired. The second leg of the flight was in daytime and I just sat reflecting on what God had done on those amazing mission journeys; wonderful memories to treasure and to share with Judy and everyone back home. I had learnt so much and been truly blessed at seeing the Holy Spirit at work in the myriad of ways He had revealed Himself. To God be the glory for the great things He has done!

Chapter 28

SURPRISES AND THE UNEXPECTED

It was 3 a.m. and once again I was on the road heading for Gatwick Airport. I was meeting up with Tim to fly to Bulgaria where we would be taking part in a tent mission. Shortly after joining the motorway I found myself in a traffic jam due to lane closures on the QE2 bridge crossing over the Thames and once I was over the bridge there were more delays on the M25. Finally, I was on clear road again and at the exit for Gatwick. What a relief – I would make the flight! My relief was short-lived as the service road to Gatwick North Terminal was jammed up. I'd never seen anything like this before. Tim was calling asking where I was as it was long past the time we had agreed to meet. I felt so bad but the best I could do was to say I would try to meet him at the departure gate and pray that the traffic would clear. Our prayers were answered as I made it to the gate at 5 a.m. just as the flight was about to close.

We arrived in Sofia and, after collecting Tim's car, made our way to his house outside Plovdiv. In the evening Tim had arranged for both of us to share at a seminar on evangelism. This was a church Tim had visited regularly on his previous mission trips and it was lovely to see the people's enthusiasm to take the word of God to others. The seminar ended at 10 p.m.; it had been a long day and we slept soundly!

The next morning we set off for Shabla in the north of Bulgaria on the coast of the Black Sea, to join the Tent 100 team led by Sofi and her husband Waldemar. Tim calculated the journey would take around eight hours so, when we stopped to fill up the car with fuel we also refuelled ourselves with coffee and a pastry. At lunchtime we met up with an English missionary couple with whom Tim had worked for a number of years. It was a well-deserved break for Tim who was doing all the driving and a great time of fellowship over our favourite Shopska salad.

It was good to finally arrive at Shabla and meet up with the team, many of whom we knew from previous mission trips. It had been another long day and we still had to travel to Kavarna, 25 miles away, where we would be based, travelling to the tent each day.

Sofi's colleague Georgi had organised the programme. Georgi's plan was to 'divide and conquer', to send me and Tim out with separate teams so that we could cover more ground. Tim's team was to go out into the villages and speak at open-air meetings. We were both assigned an interpreter for the week. Tim would be working with a very talented lady called Villy, and Sofi, who knew the area, went out with Tim and his team.

Mimi had been assigned as my interpreter, which pleased me greatly as I had worked with her before. In addition to being a fluent translator she was also a great singer and a skilled musician. Georgi was part of the team and his plan for us was to call at houses and share with people in the streets near the tent.

Shouting the Gospel in the Streets!

'Hello, I am Peter from England. I have Good News to tell you.' Dear Mimi would shout in Bulgarian whatever I said. A man sitting on his front steps waved to us and we walked down the long path to join him. We sat on the steps with him and simply shared the love of Jesus and invited him to come to the Mission tent at the end of his road.

Mimi said, 'He says he can't stand or walk.'

'Ask him if I can put my hands on his knees and pray for him.'

With the man's permission I started to pray.

The man said, 'My knees have become hot!' Then he rose carefully to his feet and started to walk around. There was a surprised look on his face. 'The pain is gone!' Mimi began to play her guitar and sang a gospel song, which brought a big smile to his face. Georgi repeated the invitation to come to the tent that evening.

We walked further down the road using the same pattern. We came to a house with a very long garden, shouting first in English followed by Bulgarian. Our team of five was invited to come down to the house. What an amazing welcome we received. We sat around the garden table with the man, his wife and his mother and Mimi began to sing. The lady of the house disappeared inside and brought us a big plate of sliced watermelon, and then went back again to get bread, homemade goat's cheese and cups of water.

We sat with them telling them quite simply that Jesus loved and cared for them. Then I asked Georgi to tell his story of how God had turned his life around and I used an old newspaper to illustrate his testimony by folding and tearing the paper until the last piece was opened up to reveal the cross. It was so evident that the Holy Spirit was at work and as all three made a commitment to follow Jesus it was wonderful to see the joy and peace and radiance on their faces. We celebrated with them as Mimi sang 'Amazing Grace'.

The man was so excited and kept repeating, 'I can feel God's love, I can feel God's love.' He wanted to have his picture taken with us and as he stood up he reached under the table and produced a pair of crutches; none of the team had realised that he was an amputee. We wanted them to come to the tent but the wife and mother were going away for a few days and he could not make the journey on his own. The family kept asking us to come back to visit them again and we promised to return in a few days with some local Bulgarian missionaries who were planning to open a church locally.

Back at the tent two of the ladies had made a big saucepan of stew and we sat around the table sharing our morning's experiences and listening to the inspiring stories from Tim's team's visit to the villages.

The opening night of the mission and Mimi and Villy led the worship. Then followed testimonies from the Bulgarian members of the team before Tim spoke. One of the people who responded to the call for salvation was a local police detective. Tim had a word of knowledge about a person who had a problem with their hand and the detective came forward again. His daughter was astounded and gasped out loud at seeing full mobility restored to her father's hand after he was prayed for. Once more, under the tent, lives were being transformed, body, soul and spirit.

165

Every morning we would gather in the tent, sharing and praying together as a team before setting out for the town. Both teams would work together handing out tracts, and Mimi and Villy would sing as we invited people from the town centre, the hospital entrance and a local park to the tent for the children's activities in the afternoon or the main event in the evening.

The second night Mimi and Villy again led the worship and then Waldemar and I shared our testimonies before Racheto, wearing traditional costume, sang some Bulgarian folk songs. It was a good evening as people responded to the message and the signs and wonders followed.

Tim and Georgi had been preaching in a nearby village that evening. The audience was mainly Muslim, which had been a bit of a surprise, but they'd had a good time.

The next evening, we rotated again and Tim was ministering in the tent. It was encouraging to see the numbers increasing as the people who had heard the Good News on previous evenings came back again bringing their families and friends with them.

Waldemar and Sofi took me out to a remote village where they had spent the day doing door-to-door evangelism. It must have been very close to the border because my phone was inviting me to accept a Romanian network. We set up our microphone speakers on the steps of a local meeting hall, the idea being that people would hear the message and music in the nearby houses. Sofi and Waldemar shared first then Racheto sang some traditional Bulgarian songs before Mimi sang 'Amazing Grace' and I shared the message. I then invited people to come and receive free Christian literature but apart from a few teenagers there was nobody in sight. It was just like speaking on the radio. In the next few minutes we saw headlights coming down the street and two or three cars pulled up to collect the material, giving Sofi the opportunity to speak with people. The evening had been very different from what I was used to but it wasn't my first surprise on the mission!

The next day Tim was out in a village in a café environment and I was back in the tent. This time I was speaking at the afternoon's meeting for young people. I had my old friend Joe Crow the glove puppet to minister to the youngsters. Joe Crow and I talked to each other, teaching the importance of having a personal relationship with God through prayer. Mimi had produced the Lord's

Prayer hand tracts in Bulgarian and these were given out to everyone. She also asked them to draw a picture of God and how they saw God and themselves, which proved to be very thought-provoking and quite a challenge.

I closed the sessions by telling the youngsters the story of the 'lost sheep' to illustrate how special each one of them was to God. It was wonderful to see them respond and pray for God to come into their lives.

That evening it was my turn to speak in the tent again and I decided to preach the same message. It was a delight to see youngsters who had responded in the afternoon back again, this time with their friends and family. At one point I looked up and noticed that the man with one leg was there; he had persuaded an uncle to bring him to the service. He had been sharing the Good News since the day Jesus met him and his face was beaming as he excitedly told everyone of the peace and love he had found.

This was Tim's and my last night in Shabla and it was wonderful to see the Holy Spirit at work as many responded for the call for salvation and asked Jesus into their lives. God had given words of knowledge and we heard testimonies of healing as people, young and old, were being touched. What a pleasure and a privilege to be part of such a wonderful team where servant hearts were so much in evidence. It was hard for Tim and I to say goodbye; the tent mission would carry on for two more nights in Shabla but we were leaving in the morning on the 500-mile drive back to Sofia.

It was a long, tiring day, especially for Tim who was doing all of the driving. We arrived at Hotel Bankya needing a meal and a good night's sleep. Tim was flying home to England early the next morning, as he had to prepare for a mission in Liverpool the following week. I had two more days in Bulgaria as I was due to speak at two churches in Sofia on the Sunday.

It was good to have a day to reflect and pray, asking God what he wanted me to share. I felt the Holy Spirit was speaking the words 'Hide and Seek'. This led me to the scripture I was to share at Sunday's meetings. Saturday evening, I was having dinner with Pastor Annie Totev and Pastor Dimitar Boukliev, the founding pastor of first Bulgarian church in London following the tent mission with Dr T.L. Osborn in England in 1999. We talked about the possibility of holding a mission in Sofia in the future. It was a wonderful evening with sincere friends who have such a passion for lost souls.

Sunday morning and I was at the House of Joy Church, which was full of many familiar faces. Pastor Emmanuel was hosting the service and leading the worship as Pastor Valdo and Borislava were on holiday. Even though the songs were in Bulgarian it didn't matter to me, as it was such a Spirit-filled time of praise. I was feeling a tremendous sense of God's presence and began to get words of knowledge: 'There is a healer in the house and His name is Jesus!' And this was before I started sharing the word. God had inspired me to share 'We are called to be salt and light' (Matthew 5:13–16) and then given me five motivation points on how to share His love with friends and family. I invited people to respond, extending it to anyone who had been touched by God. One lady immediately came forward to give testimony of how she had been healed during the service. She fell on her knees and began to prophesy. Outside the church, after the service, she told me she used to come to the church in Bishop Milcho's time; she remembered us touring Bulgaria all those years ago. It is such as privilege to serve: you don't always have to speak the language; the joy, smiles and tears say so much.

After a blessed morning we travelled across the city to have lunch with Pastor Emmanuel and his wife Silvana and mother Annie. Pastor Emmanuel asked if I would share a similar message to the morning's sermon with his own church. He also wanted me to speak about the importance of sharing a personal testimony as a believer and the importance of prayer in preparation for reaching out. It was a wonderful time of fellowship and we had a special reason to thank our heavenly Father as Silvana shared with Annie over lunch that she had been healed during the preaching in the morning service just as it says in Mark's Gospel (Mark 16:20).

That evening we met with Valdo and Borislava and their family for a meal – it was quite a gathering. It was great to be with this family of God and a lovely way to end a truly awesome ten-day mission full of surprises and the unexpected.

On Monday morning Borislava took me to the airport. It was a long day with delays, heavy rain and a bumpy flight home but I was buoyed by the news from Sofi that the final two days of the tent mission had seen yet more people saved and healed – *Slava na Boga!* – Praise God!

We travelled to London by car but parking was a nightmare. As Judy was not able to walk more than a few yards without becoming breathless, I dropped her outside the clinic and went to find somewhere to park the car. The closest space I could find was about a mile away in an underground car park.

Once back at the clinic I was allowed to sit with Judy until she was taken to be injected with the radioactive dye. She was told she could select some music to listen to whilst she was in the scanner. The scan took about an hour and once I knew she was able to come back to the waiting room I went to fetch the car.

My mobile phone battery was low so I put it into the USB to recharge. As I drove up from the car park to street level a song came out of the speaker: 'How Great Thou Art'. I knew at that moment God was at work. I couldn't wait to get back to the clinic and tell Judy. What I didn't know was she had been singing this song to herself for the hour whilst the PET scan was going on.

With the PET scan results back we found ourselves in front of a top pancreatic surgeon who was telling us it was a tumour and it had to be removed. I found myself asking him, 'Are you sure it's not a cyst?' He replied that it was too big to be a cyst and it had to be removed. Our friend Joseph Mathai, who was sitting with us, emphasised to us the importance of removing the mass as soon as possible. We looked at each other and agreed to take up the consultant's offer of doing the operation two days later on Saturday morning.

Judy and I drove into London; our friends Joseph and Sarah came by train to be with us. Judy's niece Tessmin joined us and we all came together around Judy's bed to pray before she went down to the operating theatre. One verse jumped out at me from my daily devotion and brought me such a peace and a confidence: 'Do not be afraid or discouraged . . . The battle is not yours, but God's' (2 Chronicles 20:15 NIV). We all kept bringing everything before God in prayer. It's so wonderful to have faithful friends standing alongside you at such times. 'Where two or three are gathered together in my name, I am there in the midst of them' (Matthew 18:20).

I took the lift down with Judy and walked with her to the doors of the operating theatre. The surgeon told me he would ring me the moment the operation was over but that it would take a couple of hours.

170

I re-joined Joseph, Sarah and Tessmin and we sat in a café for a while talking, drinking coffee and eating croissants. Then I felt urgency within me to go into a church and pray. Joseph, Sarah and I walked down the road and found ourselves at Southwark Cathedral. There was a service in progress but we were allowed to stand at the back. As we walked in I sensed the presence of God. It was a High Anglican service: the Bishop and clergy were chanting the Lord's Prayer and censers of incense were being swung. This was a style of worship that I wasn't used to yet I felt such peace come over me once more.

We left the cathedral and walked up onto London Bridge and stood looking up the River Thames and across to the hospital. I turned to the next page in my *Daily Light* and read these verses:

> *'Blessed is the man who listens to me, watching daily at my gates, waiting at the posts of my doors.'* (Proverbs 8:34 NKJV)

> *'Behold, as the eyes of servants look to the hand of their masters, as the eyes of a maid to the hand of her mistress, so our eyes look to the LORD our God, until He has mercy on us.'* (Psalm 123:2 NKJV)

> *'This shall be a continual burnt offering throughout your generations at the door of the tabernacle of meeting before the LORD, where I will meet you to speak with you. In every place where I record my name I will come to you, and I will bless you.'* (Exodus 29:42 NKJV)

These verses were speaking into my spirit. I read the verses aloud to Joseph and Sarah. I just had to share with them. Kevin, Judy's son, arrived asking:

'Do we have any news about Mum?'

'No, not yet. Let's go for a coffee and sit somewhere warmer. The surgeon has promised to call me.'

Eventually the surgeon called and said that everything had gone well so we strolled back to the hospital. We sat in the waiting room and time seemed to be dragging on. We had been waiting far longer than the twenty minutes we had expected to wait following the surgeon's call. Eventually I spoke to the receptionist who phoned the post-operative intensive care unit and was told Judy was still in theatre. Again, my spirit was very sensitive and I said, 'We all need to pray.' These verses came to my mind: 'Praying always with all prayer and supplication in the Spirit' (Ephesians 6:18); 'Pray without ceasing' (1 Thessalonians 5:17).

The surgeon came down to see me. He told us that the operation itself had gone well but that, due to the painkillers being administered, Judy's heart had stopped. She had responded well and was now being taken to the ICU. When we eventually got to see Judy, she was surrounded by a Spaghetti Junction-like web of pipes, drips, wires and monitors, and a very attentive medical team. The next day the anaesthetists asked if we had been praying because it was miraculous how her heart had started beating again.

Judy had asked the surgeon if, when she came out of ICU, he could arrange for her to have a room with a view. When she came out of the unit her room gave her views overlooking St Paul's Cathedral, London Bridge and the Thames. God hears our prayers in the big things and the little things.

'The steadfast love of the LORD never ceases, His mercies never come to an end; they are new every morning; great is your faithfulness.' (Lamentations 3:22–23 ESV)

Judy had the operation to remove a tumour attached to her pancreas on 31st October 2015. Twelve days later we received the good news – it wasn't cancer it was a cyst. Then the portal vein, which had blocked following surgery, miraculously responded to treatment. God answered so many prayers.

'Pray without ceasing' (1 Thessalonians 5:17) was a hallmark of our faith – seeing her at home for Christmas.

Whilst she had made an amazing recovery from the operation, Judy was not physically strong and had lost a lot of weight. She would become exhausted very quickly and breathless – the condition that was being investigated when the cyst was discovered. One morning I woke to cries for help: Judy had a pain in her chest and was extremely breathless. I called an ambulance and she was rushed to our local hospital. She was diagnosed with pulmonary hypertension and her condition was deteriorating. Once more I was praying for God to send the right doctor. A young registrar knew of the specialist unit at the Royal Free Hospital and Judy's original heart consultant had contacts to get us there. I started to research the condition on the Internet to find out more about pulmonary hypertension and ended up on a page with a picture of a doctor call Dr Benjamin Schreiber.

It was arranged for Judy to undergo tests at the Royal Free Hospital and I accompanied her in the ambulance from Romford to Hampstead. We went directly to the unit where the tests were to be carried out and handed over a bundle of medical notes to the nursing staff. Guess who was standing in the background? Yes, Dr Benjamin Schreiber.

Following some initial tests Dr Schreiber told us that Judy was seriously ill, so unwell that he didn't want her to return in the ambulance, he was going to find a bed for her on the ward at The Royal Free. In all, Judy spent two weeks undergoing tests to find out what was triggering the acute breathing problems. We thank God for the gifted medical team and medication and the vital ingredient of prayer and faith. Her recovery has been nothing short of miraculous and she still continues to surprise everyone. When she was asked if she would be a case study she agreed: 'Yes, but I have a vital ingredient – Faith – that has to be prescribed.'

> *'Faith is the substance of things hoped for, the evidence not seen.'*
> (Hebrews 11:1)

It is so important to hang on to our faith when trials come our way. Faith is a God-given gift.

Like my wife, I feel truly blessed for that God-given faith. I had a stroke and a seizure at the end of March 2016. It came totally out of the blue. I believed I was reasonably fit and strong; I had plenty of stamina. Well, at the end of March the storm hit me and I came crashing down twice in one week.

The first incident came when I went into the bathroom chasing a fly to get it out of the house and I fell back, hitting my head on the radiator. The only thing I could remember was my wife and daughter calling me, 'Peter, Peter', 'Dad, Dad,' then the paramedics arrived. I was totally disorientated. The paramedics took me to A&E where I was examined and had a CT scan. They couldn't find any damage to the brain or any underlying cause for the fall so I was sent home without any medication, even though I was still very confused.

Two days later I was talking to a friend on the phone when my speech became slurred, my mouth was dropping on one side and my left arm was becoming heavy. I realised I was having a stroke. I walked out to the kitchen to tell Judy who took one look at me and called the paramedics but not before she, with my granddaughter Dani's help, had put me in the recovery position in case I fell over. I was in an ambulance, blue lights flashing, on my way back to A&E with Susanne, my daughter, at my side. I was taken into the major incident unit. I was praying, 'Lord, don't leave me like this. Take me home or restore me. If I am here, I want be able to share the gospel and lay hands on the sick.' Praise God my mouth was working again.

This time I was given medication, my head started to clear, the left arm was no longer heavy. I was admitted to hospital and given a lot of attention: drips, scans, endless blood tests. They were trying to find the root cause and I suppose they thought that, as a missionary who had been to many different countries and visited the jungle, I might have been exposed to some exotic pathogens in my travels.

A brain scan confirmed that I had suffered a stroke but at least there is now documented evidence for those who have questioned/doubted whether I have a brain – I do indeed possess one!

I was in hospital recovering for twelve days and was soon praying for fellow patients during this time. It provided great opportunities for me to share my faith with the nurses and doctors too. The stroke consultant was so

encouraging, testing my mobility and aptitude; everything was functioning normally again. Then came a bombshell I was not expecting given the positive report from the stroke consultant: the neurologist came to tell me I couldn't drive for a year. I had to sell my car; it was a particularly difficult time as Judy wasn't yet ready to drive. It took me fifteen months to get my driving licence back.

Naturally my family came along to visit me. People knew Judy had been unwell but it surprised friends when I was unwell. The news reached people around the globe: Kevin and Leslie McNulty who had told me in Moscow on my sixty-fifth birthday that I needed to write a book, and to whom I had protested that I didn't have time, sent a message saying: 'Peter, you have time now whilst you're recovering; how about you start to write your book?'

It was like a conspiracy: three friends in ministry came in separately to visit and all three – Alan Cass, Jem Trehern and Gary Seithel – told me the same thing: 'Peter you need to write a book.' Needless to say, I asked them who had put them up to this but they all denied any collusion.

Jem in particular has continued to prompt me on a regular basis! Then one Sunday evening two of our friends from church came around. Frank and his wife Gill were sitting at the bedside when Gill suddenly said, 'Frank, I need to tell Peter something; is it alright?'

Frank replied wryly, 'How could you stop now? Whatever it is, you'd better say it.'

'Peter you need to write a book!'

This was coming from Gill, the person who is still using the Lord's Prayer bookmark, and I knew this was something I needed to do!

Maybe not being able to drive was God's way of keeping me at home so that I would finally settle down and start writing.

Once more I am reflecting on this chapter. Faith has been an important ingredient, prayer and relationship with God, love and fellowship. We certainly have friends who love us, support us in prayer and loving-kindness.

Here are the two great foundational commandments:

> *'Jesus said . . . Thou shalt love the Lord thy God with all thy heart, and with all thy soul, and with all thy mind. This is the first and great commandment. And the second is like unto it, Thou shalt love thy neighbour as thyself.'* (Matthew 22:36–39)

Over a year later I was invited to preach at Victory Church. This was the first time I had preached since ministering in Sofia and I planned to share a gospel message about the disciples facing the stormy sea. During the worship we sang 'How Great Thou Art' and the Holy Spirit came upon me; tears were running down my cheeks. My prepared message had to be set aside, and I shared the testimony of God's amazing grace to Judy and me in the preceding year, how His power had sustained us.

Chapter 30

SHOW ME YOUR WAYS, O LORD; TEACH ME YOUR PATHS

Sometimes things don't work out how you've planned, do they? Even after you've prayed and you believe you're doing God's will, some things just don't go as you anticipate.

Liberia was a mission trip I was supposed to have gone on as part of a team of four several years ago. I was all ready with my visa but ended up being disappointed because the ministry I was working with couldn't afford to send us all and decided to send my friend George and a new evangelist.

George said, 'The next time I go back, are you for up it?' We prayed and decided to do a joint venture to Liberia. We wanted to do open-air healing crusades and go into prisons, schools and hospitals, start mission school training and equipping pastors. George had always emphasised to me how poor and hurt this nation was and the humility and eagerness to learn shown by the pastors.

Initially our plan was just to travel to Liberia taking only what we could carry with us to bless the people. We began to raise support to cover the travel costs but at one of our Zeal Prayer Nights I really felt we should organise sending some aid and Bibles. I thought of hiring a 20-foot shipping container and filling it with items useful for schools and hospitals.

We wanted to do things right so when George and I visited the Liberian Embassy in London we talked about shipping the container and received real encouragement from the officials. We knew the people were very poor and many were the victims of civil war.

So now we planned to ship the container in advance so that we would arrive at the same time as the resources that we had sent. We would start our ministry campaign in Monrovia. We began collecting Bibles and aid; we had our visas ready to go. Then news came that an outbreak of Ebola was affecting the country. It soon became evident that we would have to postpone our mission.

We followed the situation on the news and we read articles on the World Health Organisation forums about how hospitals and schools had to be closed, that no public assemblies were allowed. Then came news of a second, more widespread outbreak. We decided that there was an even bigger need to help the people so we decided to actually buy a 40-foot container. We went back to the embassy again to tell them our plans.

Whilst everything seemed to be against us I still had a passion to go with George to Liberia. We both always felt we were meant to go together. Then one evening at home I opened up a magazine to an article about a doctor who had been working in Liberia with the victims of Ebola. I remember talking to God saying, 'I wish I could talk to this lady, Dr Natalie McDermott.' Just as I was saying it, the arm fell off my glasses. Thinking it just needed a new screw, the next day I called into the opticians in the high street. Unfortunately, or rather fortunately, I was told the glasses couldn't be fixed and, as my prescription was over six months old, I would need a new sight test.

I went back the next day for an appointment with Sarah, my regular optician. The test was carried out, Sarah reviewed my notes: my eyes hadn't changed. I have this habit of sharing the gospel anywhere and with anyone. Sarah asked where I had been travelling to as a missionary and where I was planning to go next.

'I was supposed to be going to Liberia, in fact I was reading an article about a doctor working with Ebola patients in Liberia and wishing I could talk to her when my glasses broke.'

'What's her name?'

'Natalie McDermott'

'That's my best friend! Give me your email and I'll ask Natalie to contact you.'

Sure enough Natalie sent me an email. It was such an encouragement knowing God had answered my cry, my prayer! It really felt like this was a 'divine appointment'. Natalie was able to share helpful information suggesting what to focus on with our aid – children, schools and orphans' needs.

I learnt time and time again that God puts people in your path. I eventually got to meet Dr Natalie when she was back in England after the Ebola outbreak was finally declared to be over. She was working with the Billy Graham organisation; her testimony was being used on their latest outreach DVD. We got to meet face-to-face and chat more about Liberia. She told me she was now working on Ebola research at Imperial College.

Listening to her testimony and then chatting to her afterwards I learnt that it was Sarah who, in their university days, had introduced her to the gospel. Once more it emphasised the importance of us all sharing our faith and 'passing the baton'. God always has a plan. I had *no* idea when my friend Gary invited me to join him at the launch of the Billy Graham DVD at a cinema in Romford that Natalie would be one of the speakers.

The response to our appeal for aid for Liberia was fantastic: Bibles, theological books, desks, bookcases, tables and chairs all for the planned mission school. Equipment for schools and orphanages: footballs, bikes, nursery items such as cots, push chairs, clothing and toys, computers and even a generator – the container was fully loaded. We were really excited and as we had bought the container outright, once the aid items had been distributed, the container would be converted into a schoolroom to teach God's word.

In the time since we had first started planning the mission we had both faced challenging ill-health situations in our families. Once more the visas weren't used. I talked to George:

'Why don't you still go?'

'No, I believe God has called us to go together,' George replied. 'Let's concentrate on sending the container, Bro.'

Can you believe we spent over a year packing it? Jumping through so many hoops to get the paperwork done before finally getting the container sealed. It spent three weeks at sea, then a year in Monrovia docks. The obstacles seemed never ending: demands for money for storage and taxes levied on charitable donations all preventing the container from being released. We

often felt frustrated and exhausted with endless conversations leading us up blind alleys. George and I continued to encourage each other: praying together and praying online with Pastor Amos, our partner in Liberia.

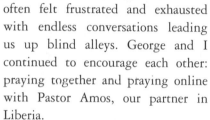

Then finally the MIRACLE happened: we received a presidential waiver on the import taxes on charitable goods. God had overruled those who sought to withhold the consignment. We are so grateful for those who continued to stand with us in prayer. Our hearts are filled with joy that so many prayers have been answered. We were so blessed that people gave so many gifts and finances and others laboured tirelessly. We give all the glory to God for this amazing mission.

It has been a blessed time seeing the photos coming through of children in schools and orphanages receiving gifts; young people and pastors receiving Bibles and theological books; evangelists receiving bikes to ride out and share the Good News.

We would have liked to make the trip but this time God used us to gather the resources so that others could use them. We continue to pray for those who will make it to heaven as a result of the project. People receive tracts and get taught from the Bible by believers who are now equipped to teach and to pass on the Good News in this vast nation which has suffered so much in the past. You've read this chapter, do pray for this wave of grace and love to fill this nation. We thank the many people who stood with us. We are so grateful to God and you.

We have learnt great lessons, I am feeling truly blessed writing these highlights, reflecting on the importance of unity, patience, perseverance, prayer and faith.

> *'Because you know that the testing of your faith produces perseverance.'*
> (James 1:3 NIV)

> *'For where two or three gather in my name, there am I with them.'*
> (Matthew 18:20 NIV)

> *'Behold, how good and pleasant it is when brothers dwell in unity!'*
> (Psalm 133:1 ESV)

GALLERY

West Ham Days

GALLERY

On a Journey

GALLERY

On a Journey

GALLERY

Tent Missions

GALLERY

Tent Missions

GALLERY

OTM BBQ Ministry

RESOURCES

Praying Hands Tract
£10.00 per pack of 100

The Way Tract
£10.00
per pack of 100

Love Tract
£10.00
per pack of 100

**Billy Bible
DVD**
£5.99 each

Zeal T-shirt
£18.00

**Passing the Baton
Book**
£9.99

You can purchase these items online. God gave the vision to develop all these items and you have read through this book.

Visit the Zeal Outreach Ministries Website
www.zealoutreachministries.co.uk/shop

We hope you enjoyed reading this book.

Contact the author.

To contact the author, please send an email to:

info@zealoutreachministries.co.uk

More information can be found online:

www.zealoutreachministires.co.uk

PASSING
the BATON
—— PETER RUCK ——

"I press toward the mark for the prize of the high calling of God in Christ Jesus." (Philippians 3:14)

Passing the Baton - defining passing of the baton as the process and act of intentionally passing on four important things - faith, hope, love and responsibility. The Great Commission is a "passing the baton" directive. When Jesus said, "Go and make disciples" He was telling those around Him to "pass it on." In other words, to pass the Good News of Jesus Christ and the important habits of faith and service in light of the Good News.

"ZEAL IS COMMITTED TO FOLLOW GOD FULLY AND TO HELP US ALL TO DO THE SAME."

ZEAL OUTREACH MINISTRIES

Peter founded Zeal Outreach Ministries with a vision and a passion to encourage others. Networking with local churches and ministries around the world, Zeal provides opportunities for training and support, inspiring others to reach out as a FATOS* and, above all, to pass the baton.

This book is a message of encouragement with the hope that you will be inspired to fulfill the purposes God has for you!

*Faithful, Available, Teachable, Obedient, Spirit-filled Servant